WHEN LANGUAGE
BROKE OPEN

EDITED BY ALAN PELAEZ LOPEZ

When Language Broke Open

AN ANTHOLOGY OF QUEER AND TRANS BLACK WRITERS
OF LATIN AMERICAN DESCENT

THE UNIVERSITY OF
ARIZONA PRESS

TUCSON

The University of Arizona Press
www.uapress.arizona.edu

We respectfully acknowledge the University of Arizona is on the land and territories of Indigenous peoples. Today, Arizona is home to twenty-two federally recognized tribes, with Tucson being home to the O'odham and the Yaqui. Committed to diversity and inclusion, the University strives to build sustainable relationships with sovereign Native Nations and Indigenous communities through education offerings, partnerships, and community service.

ISBN-13: 978-0-8165-4996-2 (paperback)
ISBN-13: 978-0-8165-4997-9 (ebook)

Cover design by Leigh McDonald
Cover art: *Racin Fon*, 2020, Didier William, Haitian American, born 1983 in Port-au-Prince, Haiti, acrylic, wood stain, ink on panel, 42 x 86 in., © Didier William, image courtesy of James Fuentes Gallery
Designed and typeset by Leigh McDonald in Warnock Pro 10.5/14 and Basteleur by Keussel, Velvetyne Type Foundry (display)

"Hurricane Marlene" by Lorraine Avila (p. 122) originally appeared in *Kweli Journal* on March 4, 2022.
"I'd Always Promised I'd Never Do Drag" by Darrel Alejandro Holnes (p. 155) is from *Stepmotherland* by Darrel Alejandro Holnes © 2022 by Darrel Alejandro Holnes. Reprinted by permission of University of Notre Dame Press.
"When Dreaming of a Future Means Letting Go" by Alan Pelaez Lopez (p. 269) originally appeared in *Teen Vogue* on October 15, 2021.
"We Never Did This to Be Beautiful" and "For the Black Kids in My 8th-Grade Spanish Class" by Ariana Brown (p. 140) originally appeared in *Sana Sana* (Game Over Books, 2020).
An earlier version of "Opening the Dominican Universe" by Alejandro Heredia (p. 235) originally appeared in *La Galería Magazine*, 2019.
"An Offering" by SA Smythe (p. 221) originally appeared in Forward Together's TDOR 2019 chapbook, *We Have Never Asked Permission to Sing: Poetry celebrating trans resilience.*
An earlier version of "Love Thy Neighbor" by Sr. Álida (p. 109) was published in the 2021 summer issue of the *Southern Humanities Review* (vol. 54.2) and anthologized in *Best Spiritual Literature* (Orison Books, 2022).
"Lido's Day" by Yamilette Vizcaíno Rivera (p. 144) originally appeared in *Places We Build in the Universe: A Latine Genre Anthology* (Flower Song Press, 2023).

Publication of this book is made possible in part by the proceeds of a permanent endowment created with the assistance of a Challenge Grant from the National Endowment for the Humanities, a federal agency.

Library of Congress Cataloging-in-Publication Data are available on the last page of the book.

Printed in the United States of America
♾ This paper meets the requirements of ANSI/NISO Z39.48-1992 (Permanence of Paper).

CONTENTS

✦

MEMORY

✦

CARE

FUTURES

✦

FOREWORD

T**HE IMPRESSIVE** book you hold in your hands is not only a labor of love, but an empowering act of self-love. Poet and scholar Alan Pelaez Lopez has graced us with this pioneering project: a community of Black trans and queer voices of Latin American descent that amplify their lived experiences and realities. But that summation doesn't do justice to the range of landscapes—intellectual, linguistic, political, and emotional—journeyed in these pages. Indeed, so much ground is covered because the gallery of entries is substantive and expansive, enriching and affective. Pelaez Lopez draws from talents across generations, identities, and nationalities to shape a startling and diverse portrait of what it means to be Black and of Latin American descent. One thing is clear, however: that these creative energies are in service to their own agency. They will be heard, especially by those who will see themselves in the language, imagery, and storytelling of *When Language Broke Open.*

Pelaez Lopez's excellent introduction provides a complete context of the anthology's scope and mission, its parameters and literary framework. It's an incisive and learned essay about a literature that has become even more urgent and necessary in this beleaguered social climate that is particularly hostile toward Black and trans people. For that reason, the University of Arizona Press and the Camino del Sol Latinx literary series are particularly proud to be a home for such a timely publication.

When Language Broke Open will no doubt be recognized for its significant literary contribution to Latinx letters, but it's important to acknowledge that the wait has been too long. Public conversations about the role and place of Black literature of the Americas have been mostly peripheral, relegated to short-lived exchanges on social media. Yet they have been happening consistently, just as Black writers and artists of Latin American descent have been exercising their creativity all along, as evidenced by this anthology. The fact of the matter is that race, gender, and sexuality challenge dialogues to become more nuanced and inclusive—expectations that even Latinx literature and scholarship have yet to catch up to. I hope that this anthology, as well as a few other recent projects showcasing Black voices of Latin American descent, signals an important change in how we perceive and engage identity when we say "Latinx."

Finally, I would be remiss if I didn't congratulate our astute and visionary editor Alan Pelaez Lopez once more. Their care and attention in curating the selections, their determination to achieve cohesion while simultaneously envisioning a panoramic compilation, and their knowledgeable introduction elevate this project to another level of literary activism and importance. In short, Alan Pelaez Lopez is brilliant—and because of that, *When Language Broke Open* dazzles with their light.

—*Rigoberto González*

ACKNOWLEDGMENTS

WHEN LANGUAGE BROKE OPEN was conceptualized and edited during a difficult and transformative time in my life. In the introduction to my chapbook *to love and mourn in the age of displacement*, I narrate my first visit to the emergency room and being bed-bound for nearly a month. Naïvely, I thought my story with hospitals and illness had ended with that poetry collection. Shortly after I began conceptualizing the call for submissions to *When Language Broke Open*, I got the sickest I have ever been. After too many doctor visits, inconclusive exams, and X-rays that revealed growing scars in my lungs, I realized I could no longer afford to be sick in the United States and moved back to my birth country. I was living in a small one-bedroom apartment in Mexico City and began an experimental treatment that consisted of about fifteen injections a month, two different inhalers, nasal sprays, dissolvable nausea pills, and vertigo medications. Some days were dreadful, and some days were decent. On decent days, I read submissions, contacted potential contributors, and met with some on Zoom to provide feedback. At the sickest moment of my life, it was the cultural production of queer and trans* Black writers of Latin American descent that energized me to make my medical appointments and administer my own injections. In other words, working on this volume offered me an escape from my material reality.

It is lonely to be trans* and disabled. Disability has offered me the opportunity to be more daring, intentional, and precise with my feelings, words, and political visions.

When Language Broke Open would not have been a possibility if it weren't for those who extended care to me when I needed it the most: Lorn Kategaya, Jaselia Gratini, Ra Malika Imhotep, Beth H. Piatote, Valeria Suarez, Ebony Bailey, Ashley Ngozi Agbasoga, Ariana Brown, Jess X. Snow, Jennif(f)er Tamayo, and my family members.

Thank you to the faculty who introduced me to the world of queer and trans* studies when I was a doctoral student at Berkeley: Juana María Rodríguez and Laura Elisa Pérez. And to Leigh Raiford for guiding me through Black studies.

As someone who had never edited a volume, I was often overwhelmed. Each contributor played a crucial role in the production of this work. They answered my questions, and when they couldn't they were honest and we troubleshot together, and some trusted me enough to consider line-by-line edits. Thank you for teaching me how to be part of a collective.

I also want to thank the team at the University of Arizona Press: Thank you for the ongoing communication throughout the entire publishing process. Thank you to Elizabeth Wilder, Leigh McDonald, Julia Balestracci, Amanda Krause, and Matt Gleeson. Rigoberto González, thank you for your commitment to the volume and for utilizing your personal research funds at Rutgers University–Newark to make sure that contributors to *When Language Broke Open* received an honorarium.

Without the scholarly and financial support of The Latinx Project at New York University, I would not have been able to finish this volume. The Miriam Jiménez Román Fellowship gave me the finances necessary to pay consultants and lift the financial burden attached to my new medications and treatment options.

While working on this manuscript, I was an assistant professor of queer and trans* ethnic studies at San Francisco State University, a program housed under the Department of Race and Resistance Studies. Thank you for your warm and life-giving affirmations Leora (Lee) Kava, Falu Bakrania, and Jaimy Mann.

And now, thank you to my current colleagues at the University of California, Davis.

INTRODUCTION

THE ACT of writing—for Black queer and trans* kin of Latin American descent—may be understood as a commitment to exploring multiple formations of the self, a direct opposition to national narratives that have been constructed on behalf of Black life. I claim this following the work of contemporary Black, queer, Latin American literary elders who have encouraged their diasporic kin to commit not only to surviving but also to honoring pleasure, joy, and rage: Ochy Curiel (Dominican Republic), Yolanda Arroyo Pizarro (Puerto Rico), and Dr. Gloria D. Wekker (Suriname). Curiel's early activism, which includes co-planning and co-hosting the Primer Encuentro de Mujeres Negras de América Latina y el Caribe (First Meeting of Black Women in Latin America and the Caribbean), left an open invitation to all Black people in the continent: to relate to Blackness, gender, and sexuality not as stagnant identities but as entry points into a politics that can help envision a future where it is easy to live. In her latest poetry collection, *Afrofeministamente*, Arroyo Pizarro suggests that what is most urgent for Black Latin Americans, Black Caribbeans, and Black Latinx people at this moment is not representation or multicultural inclusion. Instead, Arroyo Pizarro proposes that one commit to "afrosanación" (afrohealing) and "afroreparación" (afroreparation) in whatever capacity one might have, because healing and reparations are more apt to ensure a future than representation.[1] To frontload healing and reparations

---

1. Yolanda Arroyo Pizarro, *Afrofeministamente* (San Juan: Editorial EDP University, 2020).

for Black kin is to prioritize care, community, and a toolkit for how to address a Latin American and Caribbean past shaped by settler-colonial conquest and trans-Atlantic slavery. Akin to the work of Curiel and Arroyo Pizarro, Dr. Gloria D. Wekker's writings from an Afro-Surinamese, Dutch, lesbian position argue that gender and countries are never categories that can claim innocence based on their historical and political formations. With such a claim, Dr. Wekker opens a space for Black diasporic writers to name Europe's "nostalgia for empire," which helps us think more critically about the relationship that Europe still has to the Global South and Europe's investment in disciplinary power in Latin America and the Caribbean. When we do the work of thinking with and against nations and gender, larger possibilities of relationality open, activating what Dr. Wekker identifies as a feminism that is transnational, intersectional, interdisciplinary, relational, and reflective.[2] This framework is one that actively denounces ongoing organizing for trans-exclusionary feminist spaces in Latin America, the Caribbean, and their diasporas, and that makes room for a transfeminist future.

Although Curiel's, Arroyo Pizarro's, and Wekker's life-writing and theorization of gender, sexuality, the Black condition, and settler colonialism in Latin America and the Caribbean informed this project's call for submissions, the politics, stories, and testimonies that live in this anthology could never have been planned or mapped out. In fact, the title of this anthology, *When Language Broke Open*, is borrowed from a poem in the collection by Mexican American poet Irene Vázquez. In "Dispatches for a Country Without Name," Vázquez writes, "Somehow, we were most honest / when language split open." The splitting of language is the condition of possibility for finding a form of honesty that might allow us (Black queer and trans* people of Latin American descent) to construct an alternative world to the one we currently live in. The modification in this volume's title from "split open" to "broke open" declares the rupture that Black articulations manifest in Latin American and Latinx literature. In a way, this anthology breaks epistemological frameworks of race, gender, sex, sexuality, nationality, and heritage. Breaking—as a verb—is loud; sometimes "breaking" may represent an injury, and other times "breaking" signals a fugitive temporal escape from oppression and/or violence. *When Language Broke Open* makes room for us (Black queer and trans* writers of Latin American descent) to be

2. Gloria Wekker, "Still Crazy After All Those Years . . . : Feminism for the New Millennium," *European Journal of Women's Studies* 11, no. 4 (Nov. 2004): 487–500.

multidimensional beings who inherited and must work with, against, in suspicion of, and through the imagined communities of "Latinidad" and "LGBTQIA+ unity."

Despite Latin America and the Caribbean being home to the largest population of Black people outside the continent of Africa, we are written off as nonexistent. I am careful with my language and say "written off" because Latin Americans know that Black people in Latin America exist. Some non-Black Latin American entities choose to adapt, carry, and retell a narrative of the Americas in which Black life is absent. The experience for people of Latin American descent who were born and grew up in the United States (Latinx) is different because Latinidad in the United States is shaped by U.S. federal immigration law, census data-tracking methodologies, and the ways in which U.S., Latin American, and Caribbean media circulate and narrate "Latinidad."

As a Latin American writer, I know that Black people of Latin American descent have been strategically written out of culture, society, and politics, because, as I edit this anthology from Mexico City, I take breaks to walk down the corridors of my neighborhood. In under a week of editing breaks, I have spotted a costume store named "El Negrito" and a restaurant named "La Morena" depicting a Black woman with lips larger than her face, and on two occasions the police have asked me for my "documentos" because I cannot possibly be a national of the country I was born in. These moments disclose a national consciousness that "negritos" and "morenas" exist in the country, while at the same time the police identify Black diasporic peoples as foreigners and/or irregular migrants in our own countries of birth. Racial profiling across Latin America gives non-Black people in Latin America permission to caricature and exploit narratives, images, and stories about who (or worse, *what*) Black people are. These biases and denials of Black personhood migrate to the United States, strengthening and enforcing already racist and anti-Black tropes about *all* Black people regardless of nationality, Indigenous affiliation, and ethnic and culture-specific identities, which makes growing up a Black person of Latin American descent in the United States an experience that is difficult to articulate and difficult to find a consenting audience to whom to render it.

Black people of Latin American descent know that nation-states do not protect Black people, and therefore the notions of a united "Latin American" and "Latinx" identity fall apart when speaking and thinking about quotidian Black experiences. Ecuadorian poet Andrea Alejandro Freire F. writes, "Todo lo que / escribo, lo escribo / desde la imposibilidad / de apalabrar mi existencia. / Mi monstrua, negra / y precaria existencia." Cuban American writer Jessica Lanay translates their words as, "All that I / write, I write / from the impossibility / to speak for my existence. / My monstrous, Black / and precarious existence." In their writing, Freire F. teaches us that Latin American countries, just like the United States, surveil language, and that each individual country (with their surveillance technology) determines both socially and legally acceptable gender and racial categories. As a Black, trans*, and HIV-positive person from Latin America, Freire F. lives as a legal impossibility, since Black trans* people are not afforded rights parallel to those of cisgender, heterosexual, non-Black citizens. Because a trans*, Black, HIV-positive person of Latin American descent cannot be legally imagined, the everyday material conditions of someone who lives at the intersection of those realities is often branded as unreal and nonexistent. As a result, language and culture must fall apart for a space of articulation to be carved out and attended to. That articulation manifests in the poetry, essays, fiction, creative nonfiction, and graphic art that live in *When Language Broke Open*.

In "An Offering," Costa Rican–Jamaican poet SA Smythe, almost as if speaking with Freire F., writes, ". . . in case language doesn't express desire, but hides it, / You must remember to reach only for the neither thing, / To be righteously unashamed of this grief until the otherwise comes / Until that time when we may name ourselves whole, if not holy, / And stop eulogizing the project of living long enough to see / That it has yet to come, and so can never die." Writing in both an ancestral and a contemporary voice, Smythe asks Black trans* kin to invite, reach for, and linger with "the neither thing." This tender reaching for "the neither thing" feels like an attempt to reach that which has been discarded and/or made to feel small in our lives. When engaging in the act of reaching for "the neither thing," Smythe poetically theorizes, we realize that the "project of living . . . has yet to come," but it doesn't mean that we've never lived. As many Black trans* artists, activists, and trailblazers have taught us, aliveness is temporal, and if we want to be alive every day, we must pledge to reach out and forward to "name ourselves whole, if not holy." Echoing Smythe, Boricua poet Jeydelyn Martinez writes, "There is no such thing as liberation without grief," indexing the fact that liberation is not a utopian concept, but a vision grounded in a material reality that refuses to hold freedom and grief as mutually exclusive. Perhaps we will experience some of our freest moments amid our collective and individual grieving.

Split into three parts—"Memory," "Care," and "Futures"—*When Language Broke Open* practices Smythe's offering of reaching out and forward and Martinez's attention to grief. In the call for submissions, I asked, "How do queer and/or trans* Black writers of Latin American descent address memory? What are the textures of caring, being cared for, and accepting care as Black queer and/or trans* people of Latin American descent? And how do queer and trans* embodiments help us understand and/or question the past and the present, and construct a Black queer and trans* future?" Through these interrogations, I sought new engagements with memory, care, and time that centered on Black queer and/or trans* writers of Latin American descent. While the call for submissions pre-thematized the anthology, the work submitted gave the anthology shape in the form of testimonio (a subgenre of Latin American literature popularized by Miguel Barnet's 1996 text *Biografía de un cimarrón*) and what Costa Rican–Jamaican writer Quince Duncan coined as "afro-realism," which is the practice of living one's own word.[3] For Duncan, afro-realism is the ability to take experience and shape it into fiction without reproducing the expected narratives that non-Black Latin American and Caribbean audiences demand from Black writers. Duncan explains that afro-realism is "a construction and reconstruction of reality, without ceasing to be fiction, without losing the sense of fantasy that makes us feel delight when reading it."[4] Through the lenses of testimonio and afro-realism, the contributors to *When Language Broke Open* allow us to relate to memory, care, and time in ways that are always already seeking accountability, demanding an audience as in a court of law, and plotting alternative visions of Black queer and trans* futures that do not compete with each other but complement one another.

The logistical process of this manuscript felt like a testimony to itself. When the call for submissions went out on social media, writers were excited, confused, and provoked. Emails with questions about what constituted "Latin American descent" came in. A writer born in Trinidad and Tobago wrote asking if they would be considered Latin American or Latinx as someone whose ancestors migrated from Venezuela to Trinidad and Tobago. There were numerous Haitian American writers asking if they met the qualifications to submit since they shared the same island

3. See A. Cruz-Malavé, "Testimonio," in *Keywords for Latina/o Studies*, ed. D. R. Vargas, L. La Fountain-Stokes, and N. R. Mirabal (New York: New York University Press, 2017); and Dorothy E. Mosby, *Quince Duncan: Writing Afro–Costa Rican and Caribbean Identity* (Tuscaloosa: University of Alabama Press, 2014).

4. Translated from the Spanish. Original in Quince Duncan, *Un señor de chocolate: Treinta relatos de la vida de Quince*, 1st ed. (Heredia: Programa de Publicaciones e Impresiones, Universidad Nacional, 1996).

as the Dominican Republic, a clearly canonized Latin American country. I affirmed each email and encouraged submissions. Some submitted; some did not. I outline this process because it speaks to the language of "Latinidad," "Latin America," and "Latinx" splitting open, resurrecting an intellectual inquiry posed by (non-Black) Cuban American critic José Esteban Muñoz in 2000: "How is it possible to know Latinidad?"[5] In asking for contributors who self-identify as "Black queer and/or trans* writers of Latin American descent," the volume calls for a transnational diasporic community as opposed to a strict U.S., Latin American, or Caribbean Spanish-speaking community. This verbiage makes space for political exiles who may no longer be considered "nationals" of their home countries, transnational adoptees and other writers who grew up without their biological parent(s) or immediate communities, and writers whose everyday life has been shaped by what Frantz Fanon names "l'expérience vécue du Noir" (the lived experience of Blackness)—famously mistranslated as "the fact of Blackness"—and for whom Blackness has therefore become the central analytic through which we see the world, as opposed to an analytic that first thinks in terms of nation, culture, or a deracialized hemispheric lens.[6]

The writing in *When Language Broke Open* reveals the messiness, nuance, and magnitude of Black queer and/or trans* life. Sometimes, we are there for one another. Other times, we are not. We live, we project, we fuck up, we reflect, we change, we are changed, and we dream of change. Edited and organized as a kitchen-table conversation, *When Language Broke Open* lets go of the constant need to explain who we are. Instead, we entertain who we were, who we are now, and who we may or may not be tomorrow, and all those considerations are of equal importance. In claiming back our narratives, memories, experiences, and imaginations, we defend our right to speak. More specifically, we reject the surrogate storyteller that has been used in the field of Latinx and Latin American poetics, Latinx and Latin American literature, and "Hispanic" literature. We no longer encounter Black queer and trans* characters written through the gaze of what in some Latin American and Caribbean nations is referred to as a "blanca/o mestiza/o" and "euromestiza/o" who is also cisgender and heterosexual. Here, you encounter those of us who have always been Black, some who actively resist any easy categorization under the binaries of the

5. See José Esteban Muñoz, "Feeling Brown: Ethnicity and Affect in Ricardo Bracho's 'The Sweetest Hangover (and Other STDs),'" *Theatre Journal* 52, no. 1 (2000): 67–79.
6. See Frantz Fanon, *Peau noire, masques blancs* (Paris: Éditions du Seuil, 1952).

LGBTQIA+ alphabet, and those of us who move in and out of identities so that our goals are future-oriented as opposed to identity-centered. Blackness is a condition, a politics, a commitment to a people, and a way of life. Queer and trans* embodiments may represent feelings, experiences, politically produced statuses, and words that continue to shapeshift as often as the world does. Latin American heritage names a location our ancestors arrived at and/or departed from, and under a white-supremacist world system, acceptance by and legibility to a Latinx and Latin American imagined community is not our destination. Latinidad is a throughway from where we can speak and where we can choose exits that are more liberating than the narratives and roads we have been told to reproduce and follow as Black diasporic peoples, some who may never be able to trace an origin.

When Language Broke Open is an invitation to let go of all we have inherited so that we can make space for new inheritances and learn to choose which of our past inheritances speak to our values and visions. *When Language Broke Open* is a dialectical space, a party, a ceremony, a family fight, a room to grieve and laugh in simultaneously, and always a vision for a world-otherwise.

—*Alan Pelaez Lopez*

.

WHEN LANGUAGE
BROKE OPEN

Another Diaspora Poem

IRENE VÁZQUEZ

Diaspora Poem speaks of beaches
I have never
set a single foot on, says sprinkle
in some words in Spanish so they know
you have something to remember;
Diaspora Poem says watch
me, says you must be proof
the subaltern can speak,
says always yell, says stay
yelling; Diaspora Poem says
wandering is better than any home
you could settle into, says you were denied
the past so keep pushing
toward the future, says yearn,
says drink up though you will never
be filled; Diaspora Poem says lie down
for me, cuts out my tongue
so I know
what it means to lack, says isn't it glamorous?
Isn't the loneliness worth it?
Says let them see you cry in public
so they know you're a poet, says
anyone who calls you cliché is an anti-
immigrant bigot; Diaspora Poem calls me baby,
sings me to sleep
at night since no one else will,
Ella canta las mañanitas
que cantaba el Rey David;
Diaspora Poem never says

sorry,
calls me bitch and queen
out the same mouth,
says I am your home now, says this
is your home now, says die
a martyr like Selena, says
you were born for this,
but all I can muster is
no landscape
is forever, I can only stand
where my feet are, even when I'm dying
of thirst, even when there are too many
maps to make sense of,
and I'm too turned around to find
the place I've never had the words
to call home,
so I call collect,
ask my Abuelita to keep pushing pesos
into the booth,
ask her to stay on the line until
I can form sentences in my mother tongue,
tell her,
te quiero
tanto, te extraño,
vamos a ir a México pa' mis vacaciones
de invierno,
but all I can manage is *I'm sorry,*
and not even in Spanish either,
so I pray to nuestra virgen that I'll
survive another winter,
in the meantime,
I dream of the last time
I felt fluent
in any language,
of the last year I didn't need a passport
to cross the border,
of all the nights
walking home from the circus
when I'd make it to the front gate,

right where the buganvilla
bloomed and she'd call me
hijita de mi vida,
and I wake up gasping,
wondering if I will pass on
all this longing to my daughter's
daughter too, if she will remember the taste
of limonada in the summertime,
or if she too will be trapped
in this world without end,
because I can't help myself,
my body was born
for warmer climates, but I didn't know that
until I moved up North,
until I felt my chapped lips
burn when the cold
sets in
no matter how much coconut oil
I rub on,
so when it keeps snowing
into April,
I get on my knees at Easter
service sobbing *I will pay*
any price to evoke
the unnameable,
and all the voices
in my head
speak of beaches, speak of deserts, speak
of homelands, then at once
go silent,
or maybe speak
all as one, saying
we knew it,
we were right
all along.

MEMORY

When One Door Closes, Another Door Flows

EHQS / IZAR

EPISODE #1: SUMMER 2020

A**S I** sat on a NJ Transit bus heading to my cousin's house for dinner, I found myself daydreaming about my journey through San Ignacio, Belize, during the fall of 2019 and the spiritual homecoming I experienced there. I remember the way the land greeted my body, in a warm, tender, easeful embrace, continuing to reverberate to this day, perhaps pointing to the fact that I will inevitably return. This electric connection has happened in other geographies I have moved through, and every time I feel the spark I am reconnected to my spiritual core and energetically reminded of past lives lived.

Traversing Belize came about through a choreographic artist residency I self-curated where my intention was to travel to my ancestral homelands of Guatemala and Belize, tune in to subtle frequencies, and develop a performative work as a culmination of my experience. I invited Jennifer, a dear friend I had met in Nicaragua many years prior, to support me along my journey. Jennifer became a solid pillar of support as I visited family, connected with queer artists on the ground, and tapped into the Africanist presence that exists within my lineage. I had originally designed the residency to last one to two months, but due to performance commitments in the United States I had to cut the trip short, which inhibited me from traveling to Livingston and Puerto Barrios, Guatemala, which is where the Afro-Guatemalan Garifuna communities are based.

The time spent with Jennifer became a heart-centered, shadow-work-excavation healing retreat. We dug deep into the crevices of each other's hearts, laughed, cried, shared aspects of our truth, and became salves for one another as elements of our wounds reared their heads. The two-week residency also became a tender encounter with the site of ancestral grief. The grief made me feel out of sync, out of body, out of time, in time, and as this process unfolded, what heightened the grief was my underlying desire to seek affirmation that I belonged there and a sense of homecoming from the landmass of Guatemala, which I had experienced before in other terrains. But the affirmation and welcome never came. I felt dissonance, discomfort, and a need to hide, rest, fall apart.

"Trust and surrender to the process. Trust in the resistance. Trust in the discomfort and allow yourself to be changed from within," my ancestral guides said.

Jennifer came with me to visit my mom's side of the family while I was on this residency because I didn't want to do it alone, especially as a queer body. When around my blood family, I never know what to say; I feel awkward, out of place, a deep sense of nonbelonging emerges alongside an opening of the heart depending on how I'm received and loved up on. This tension is sweetly complex. There is always the slight pressure and fear that some aspect of my sexuality would need to be revealed, explained, defended. As much as I desired to open up to the family that chose to stay in Guatemala about my sexuality, I wasn't able to, because the assumption that I would be received with judgment outweighed the desire to open up. This dynamic had forced me to develop a mechanism of protection where I became impenetrable stone: nothing coming in, nothing coming out. My prayer for my heart is to erode these walls and allow myself to be seen, held, and heard no matter where in the world I go.

On my grandmother's ninety-first birthday gathering, I called my mother on FaceTime. As I held the phone in front of my grandmother's eyes and we all sang "Happy Birthday," I heard my mother crying. I could suddenly sense the root cause of the unshakeable sadness I had been feeling for such a long time. The sadness was and was not my own. I fell into how hard it must have been for my parents to have left their own families behind when they decided to migrate to the United States. I, too, have had to shift geographies for different reasons, yet the underlying intention has always been to create queer constellations and ecosystems that would be strong enough to hold me through times of celebration, times of need, and times in between.

As someone born in the United States, I find that the energetic bound-aries I wish to uphold with my blood family always become slightly skewed, because I feel a responsibility to support them that comes from Latinx conditioning of *needing* to be family oriented, and although aspects of my upbringing do align with my current value system, I am clear that I need to continuously prioritize my own boundaries, needs, growth, healing, and evolution first and foremost. It is from this place of abundance that I am able to be of service to those around me. The more I focus on my personal growth and healing, the more this impacts those within and outside of my lineage. I am clear that I am not here on this planet to fulfill the expecta-tions others have of me. I am here to become more and more myself, and, like with anyone else in my life, trust needs to be earned and my boundaries need to be honored.

My grandmother on my mother's side grew up in Izabal, Guatemala. I've had so many questions for my grandmother, yet whenever I'm around her nothing comes out. I freeze and I don't know why. My mother is always telling me that she always asks for me when they talk on the phone, and I feel stuck when it comes to building a bridge between us. Do I have to? What if our relationship exists in the realm of the unseen and unspoken? The little bit that I know about my ancestral lineage comes from excerpts my mom and aunties share with me about their lives in moments when I've returned home from my travels. I listen and hold space.

I feel a paradoxical tension knowing that AfroIndigenous blood runs through me yet not being able to pinpoint exactly who my peoples are, what our rituals, dances, songs, medicines are. On my dad's side, however, I was able to trace our paternal line to the Mbundu peoples of Angola. I am aware that the illusion of separation and isolation is a lie that colonialism and white ideologies want me to believe, the illusion that I am fragmented, broken, separated from my roots. Now I know that I have never been and never will be disconnected. As a mover, choreographer, performer, I acti-vate the wisdom stored in my bones and DNA through my movement. This wisdom seeps into my life in unexpected ways and makes itself visible, yet the ancestral connections always remain elusive, ephemeral, and opaque. Am I willing to be okay with where I'm at in my process? The hardest part of this process is when blood relatives make anti-Black or anti-Indigenous statements, as if these same presences did not run through their own veins. I source compassion for them, though, because their ignorance has been passed down, has been inherited. I've beat myself up in the moments when I couldn't source the courage to speak up and remained silent. The silence revealing the gap between the academic and woke circles I am a part of and my own family's intergenerational lived reality. Choosing which battles to go into and which to let go is an active practice in my life.

Silence. Unspoken. Silence. Is Broken. In order to break the spell of silence, I am required to speak my truth and defend the things that I believe in.

What has happened to their hearts, psyches, and bodies after twenty-eight-plus years of living in the United States? I notice the ways in which the hyperindividualization of the American dream permeates our family and I wish it were different. When I talk with my parents, they always mention that they have never really felt at home in the States. The journey of securing their citizenship was so arduous, involving court dates and deportations, that I wonder if overcoming this hardship is what keeps them here. And then there are also the unspoken truths of abuse and harm that permeate and remain unspoken.

Is it my responsibility to press unmute? Whose responsibility is it?

Trigger Warning: Mentions of childhood sexual abuse (CSA)

A mí me gusta andar con pelo sueltx.

I grew up and came of age during a time when my parents and several family members were undocumented. We attended a highly conservative Pentecostal church Sundays, Tuesdays, and Fridays.

Every week. Imagínate.

The beginning of the shame chronicles: being told this and this and this was wrong, unacceptable, dirty, y si haces esto te vas para el infierno! I was saddened to see how these biblical rules kept pushing all of the youth, including myself, out of the holy sanctuary, as we attempted to model a spiritual perfectionism that was not possible to achieve. I used to sing my heart out in church, giving sermons and feeling cute, until I felt the acidity of the homophobic pedagogy being spewed and quickly realized there was no space for me there. The church was also the space where I had been sexually harmed, and this compounded my discomfort and distrust, and propelled my so-called descent from all things related to God. I allowed shame to sever me from my connection to the Divine and never returned to that church space because it was not possible to create structures of accountability there. It took me years to realize and understand that I had never been disconnected from the Divine and that I was now choreographing my own relationship to Spirit in a way that centered my queerness, choreographic rituals, and movement, and that radically divested from performative and heteronormative toxic dogma.

There was a conversation I had with my mother a while back in which she mentioned my great-grandfather, who apparently was a musician, Black, and whom I had never heard of up until then. I wish I remembered his name. Perhaps this is where my love for movement and all things sonic stems from? I have hesitated to claim my own Blackness and Indigeneity within the context of the United States because of the history of slavery and genocide that is specific to this geography. I only have clips of stories to hold that are not even my own to hold on to . . . slippery assemblages. The specificity of the experience of Black folks who are descendants of the trans-Atlantic slave trade is also one that I cannot claim. Yet aligning myself with my Blackness and claiming this presence as it relates to my Guatemalan roots does feel important as a way of centering Black lives and therefore my own. So what do I do with the resistance that shows up? What would change if I started to show up for myself even more? How do I claim my Blackness in a culturally competent way with so many missing pieces of information? Do I belong, and if so, where do I belong? Why does geographic place feel so critical to unpacking this sense and nonsense of belonging? What happens when lineages claim me? What have I inherited? What am I ready to let go of?

During my residency, I had wanted to interview and talk with queer Guatemalan artists to hear about their work and exchange survival strategies and pleasure practices. Sadly, I fell super ill on the evening when the annual queer party was happening, so I was only able to interview two folks, a writer and a dancer/performer. I caught glimpses of their lives over bad Chinese food, as we danced to old pop songs in a gay bar near Guatemala City's Central Park and shared intimate stories of our artistic work over cold beer. Secretly, I was glad that I wasn't able to go to the annual queer party because, as a low-key, high-key introvert who is now sober, I have recently found traversing queer spaces more challenging. What would the experience of moving through a slower-paced club space look and feel like? I realized that I would need to spend more time in Guatemala to understand how queer and AfroIndigenous presences revealed themselves and intersected.

As I continued along my journey, the energetics of Guatemala City and Tikal/Flores, which I visited on the second half of my trip, did not feel like strong matches for me either. Too many tourists running around sacred spaces felt off, and I recall hearing this white woman at the top of one of the pyramids say, "OMG . . . The ruins in Mexico are *so much better.*" The comment broke my heart; made me, as a descendant of this landmass, feel not good enough. I left that day with a feeling of gnawing teeth that made my skin crawl. I imagined pushing her off the pyramid as a sacrificial lamb and was left wondering what it would be like to return and traverse the space alone without interruption.

It wasn't until I crossed over into Belize to connect with a queer couple who run an arts space in San Ignacio called ArtZmosphere that I finally began to feel at home. As soon as I stepped off the bus and walked over to meet Steph at a local restaurant in San Ignacio, I could feel the frequency of the earth below my feet change and welcome me. Flow became immediate and I felt like I was receiving some kind of clue regarding my ancestral connections; cellular corporeal effervescent knowledge becoming exposed. In every interaction thereafter, folks on the street asked me for directions or confused me with their family members and old friends. This sacred recognition created the feeling of belonging that I had expected to experience in Guatemala. There were pupusa spots, Caribbean and Chinese restaurants all within a block of where I was staying, and the beautiful energy of the Caribbean Sea was palpable. All of this felt familiar, felt like home, even though I had literally just landed there. The cherry on top was that I could finally allow my butthole to relax and unclench after weeks of being in Guatemala feeling like I needed to watch my back constantly. Sadly, I was only able to spend about thirty-six hours in Belize before catching my flight back to Oakland the next day.

Within that short timespan, I will never forget that on the way to the airport, I felt a voice tell me that if I wanted to, I could get off the van and stay in Belize, and that everything would work out. It felt ridiculous to imagine myself staying, since I didn't have anything planned for my time there. I had commitments to see through in the United States, and what would happen if I didn't show up? I had been through moments like this before where a portal was opening in the form of an invitation to stay and it was up to me to say yes or no. This moment had happened before when I had been living abroad in Berlin.

A part of me still wonders what would have happened if I had stayed, but I assuage that sensation by remembering that I can return and that what was waiting for me will still be there for me even if I return in ten years. Belize is a young, beautiful, and emergent country that feels like home because it contains the Central American, Mayan, and Caribbean vibes that, combined, engender a sense of belonging for me.

From my corporeal understanding, Guatemala, as a landmass, seems to be holding a lot of trauma that needs to be addressed considering the U.S.-sanctioned and funded genocide against Indigenous communities that happened there. As an empath, an intuitive healer, and someone with ancestral connections to Guatemala, I could literally feel the weight of the troubled waters and history as I moved throughout the landscape.

I also wondered about what my life would have been like if my parents had decided not to migrate to the United States and what it would be like for no one to need to migrate because all geographic ecosystems are nourished, abundant, and not forced to be in codependent relationships with exterior world powers. What if we located world power within our own bodies?

There is a deep frustration and anger that I feel when I consider how the forces of Christianity, colonialism, white supremacy, and capitalism literally destroyed the Mayan archives and cosmological ways of being. This trip made crystal clear how the reverberations of this destruction continue to this day and have added to my internal sense of un/belonging in this Central American–American topography. How do I relinquish this anger and transform it using my creative energy and Spirit? Am I proud to be Chapinx? What elements of these identities serve me? How do I use language to create an identity that doesn't implement the language of the oppressor, that is spacious enough to hold my multiplicity and process of becoming? How do I create containers that allow for grief to emerge, be witnessed, and act as a catalyst for my individual and our collective liberation? How can I trust that being present, showing up, listening, and asking questions is more than enough? How can my presence support the land with its own healing process?

Traversing Belize activated these questions and provided the opportunity to map the places where I have felt this frequency of belonging as part of a longer-term ancestral, artistic, and spiritual project. I aim and pray to head back to Belize, Guatemala, El Salvador, Mexico, Costa Rica, and Nicaragua as ancestral hot spots that will support me in unearthing new aspects of my lineage and unique spiritual gifts. I remain open to communing, specifically with my queer, trans, nonbinary ancestrxs, past, present, and future, to guide me along the path of surrendering to the unknown.

Home

SA SMYTHE

He left our house,
after giving me tools
all the tools to forge
our future in the world:

a cleaver smooth as water,
a knife quick as wit,
an oven cast in night.

I gave mother the tools
those precious forlorn tools and asked,
Can we make a home with these?

She taught me how to braise,
how to chop, how to cut
I showed her all the sense my hands knew.

My mother taught me the worth
of a word so not just anyone
could wander in my door,

and I haven't always known
when to speak, but when I do,
my song is sharp and dark,

it's a river spilling off my tongue
into an ocean rising between me
and any house that tries to keep me
from my own

y volver volver

SA SMYTHE

just got back & i already feel the need to time travel again
not the way that white folks love to fetishize
its possibilities: the chance to touch everything,
say they were there,
                            spread their imperiousness
           across every dimension

what even is whiteness
if not the ultimate butterfly effect?
            except all the butterflies are undead
            actually, emaciated moths
            & made of stone
wherever they land,
                            it's yours
whose flesh they infect
& turn inside out
you who they made believe the world
was nothing but monarchs

i don't need that kind of time travel
never wanted to be blue, the fifth element,
the poor *baboso* with the ridged forehead
using militarized hand gestures,
the madman in comically long scarves
whizzing around alone for centuries in a telephone box

i want to do it the kindred way,
dizzying along my own time stream,
wrenched sideways from oblivion
back to 2012 so i could say *no*

& never know the treachery of hwy 17
or the genders i left there
back to 26 december 2010 so i could say something
like *let go*
but don't let go tata, my love—
does it hurt?
                    i want back to september 2001   to may 1965
                        to december 1948   to september 1984
                august 1962
                    july 1960
                                            1821

                to 1493
some shit like that   (there's the fetish,
                i knew it would come) i want *then*,
congealing right there in the 60s
so i could tell my father
                        to get off that plane. i'd say,
                        turn back around not-yet-daddy,
tell him how things are better in limón
        how it's hard but you'll miss yourself in the end
        how they'll do their best to break you
        so let's just stay in the fields. *we can build here*
        but my hands are becoming apparitions

i would have reappeared, embraced
in the shadows of the broad welsh beech trees
in the middle of whispering to my mother
how she doesn't need to stay
remember that i plead, there
under her childhood bed
materializing at night once the candles go out,
preparing her for a life
of letting go too soon

i will have raced through throngs
                        of dark young men
in wide-brimmed hats & too-long neckties
queued up along the kingston docks,
want to thrust myself

into my un-grandfather's arms june 1948
& beg him not to do it
get the fuck off the boat, Mas Wilmott,
don't do this to us, the future
was always already here   but i'm stuck
        & not so sure anymore

flight attendants call up security
as my father kisses abuela & tia maria
& steps on the plane,   the windrush men
brush me off my grandfather because i'm debris
but i show them then i leave
an imprint of tears & snot & blood—
nailbeds still bleeding—
like the shroud of turin on his sunday best
can see madge shooing me out of my mum's house,
& i'm rabidly clawing at the floor
as they pull me by my legs out from under the bed

it was always like that, always bringing me back here. like a moth to a
flame
headfirst to the moon

                        unable to save us or the others,
                        waiting to undo myself again—

Held together by an ocean breeze

LITTLE WREN

my tongue fumbles over words
      words missed
      words forgotten
      words lost.

I speak to my ancestors in a language they never met.
they speak back in words I'll never uncover.

there's a certain sadness of it all. the building and rebuilding of my people. we cleanse ourselves in the ocean because that's where our tears lie and that's where we are understood.

we are island hoppers. survivors. the weed that cannot be tamed or squashed. the pinnacle of evolution, that seeing and knowing that even in the heat of a concrete jungle, we can grow and flourish.

my strength comes from them as a wave from a breeze 50 yards back. we never met, yet here I am. rebuilt and molded beyond the structures they met, yet the confines are so similar, even with another name.

I can taste the beginnings of freedom, did they smell it? or did they crave its embrace so viciously they crashed into the ocean to taste it?

I miss a world from years and years ago. yet I know my people weren't perfect. neither am I. neither are we. we're island hoppers. we survive. and we love the ocean.

I don't claim too much. one can get only so far removed from a people that one's memory becomes dreams.

my blood knows though what my tongue can't bear to carry. a language lost, transformed to another and shoved down like a bitter mush, to another bitter meal.

how can I say I love you?

how can I say I'll carry your memory? whole stories were blurred across the Caribbean, then states, followed by pain only your family knows how to pierce open. so much got lost in the process of survival. yet when I feel myself move to the clave I know only my blood could cause that. and my tongue craves what my people do. the brain forgets what the heart remembers. and while we try to survive the culture remains.

teach me how to honor you at the ocean when I go to wash away my fears. I will. with my fumbling tongue and ways I will chip at this shield I built from water, flour, and a bitter determination to return to you and I will show my love in each and every way until we forget I even left.

Red Clay

LITTLE WREN

my earth is red clay
sticky and languid.

when I was young, I would plunge
my fingers into the earth and search

my arms would pierce with an urgency
let me get rooted.

nature has a way of knowing what
you are too scared to say.

the earth would grab around my
arms and hug, securing me for a

moment. but I would get called
back into the house.

I would feel the ground tugging against
my separation. I was another daughter
taken.

how unwise. a condemned migrant,
taken from a home that no longer
remains,
walking away from shelter.

Haiku for Great-Grandma Coolie

(from generations)

TIRZAH SHEPPARD

Puckered soft wet lips
Cloud of wrinkly brown skin
Bowl of peppermint

From behind the kitchen curtain
We hear the chants
Bambity bambity, oh lawd

When we ask "Cools, what ya cookin' for lunch?"
Your sharp tongue sings
Yuh mudda balls an' yuh fadda *pum pum*

You spit on the pavement
Where I must kneel on a grater
If I don't return home before it dries

A series of dream visitations
I collect and recycle memories
To piece together a you for me

To Grandma 'Nita

TIRZAH SHEPPARD

Sometimes I think about the nights I don't remember
Retold stories that I've carefully hoarded over the years
I wonder how you would fit into my life now

I have no scent to remember you by
But when I close my eyes I feel your presence
Like warm humidity kissing my cheeks

Every spring we bake a cake in your honor
And as the calendar passes over your birthdate,
I'm reminded to worry about the security of this overutilized password

Every now and then I stumble upon a forgotten memory
I pick it up, gripping it with clammy hands
Afraid it will be permanently lost should I put it down again

Shake it Señorita . . .
I hum,
Desperate to remember your face.
Concentrating, I look out from my car seat
But when I look up all I see is your framed portrait from our living
room

At 7, I lie in bed with my mother as we read aloud together
Suddenly her breath is heavied and shallowed
I feel her chest tremble and I see her face drenched in tears
How does one console their mother?

"To Miss Tirzah Danielle From Grandma 'Nita"
You wrote

I wind up the music box
Yet again mesmerized by the comb grazing the pimpled pin drum
I divert my attention to your handwriting
Stroking the faded sticker as warm droplets form on my face

Rainbow Rosary

TIRZAH SHEPPARD

My mother
Hands me
A plastic
Rainbow
Rosary

Coolie wanted you to have this
She decides

I roll the beads
Between my fingers
As I wonder
If Coolie
Somehow
Foresaw my queerness

"Creo que mi bisabuela era bruja" I whisper

Hoo Doo Interests

ALLISON WHITTENBERG

MaMa Fontaine stirs gumbo in a big rusty pot
telling me that joy is squashing a pregnant roach.
She is a jailbird,
an ex–lounge singer,
and a literary agent (who won't sign me).
She wonders if it is just some quirk,
or does insanity truly run parallel to our family.

I count the sky's stars under a non-tropical
night on Harriet Island, but I am reminded of nothing.

PaPa Fontaine shoots his mouth off
like a blind man with a pistol.
Yakking about some cataclysmic battle,
lying about being John . . . St. Kitts . . . Wayne,
the outlaw Cowboy of the Caribbean.
A sea lion land-locked, he is presently unemployable.

He longs to go back to his island,
but MaMa is too Americanized to get with that.

The criminal glam that they were both in.
The corrosive anti-culture.
A self-stroking soul world.
A milling population of pimps and chippies.
Con men and preachers.
Matriarchs and gaudy prophets.

A neo hoo doo manifesto that is not in the travel brochures.

Tourist only ride the tame horses.
They honeymoon at the Holiday Inn
where the sky meets the sea.
They say "How about that bobsled team . . . Ha Ha."
Yet my folks will never go back to Jamaica
and make it their own.

Watching Jordan's Fall

ALLISON WHITTENBERG

. . . God, I hate November
All the hope I had hoped
Against hope for Jordan.

Dad beat Jordan, to
Straighten him out, to show
Jordan, to silence him.

My brother lived until the next
Season, on to the next winter,
Very quiet like a fallen leaf.

From Under Crack Rock

Surviving the Reagan Years

LOUIE ORTIZ-FONSECA

M Y MOTHER began smoking crack in the summer of 1986. At that time, it was widely known as "crack rock." I was nine years old and I already had mastered the art of secrecy. I didn't call it art or survival; it was just life under the "rock." I learned many things that summer that would forever change me.

I learned to check the spoons for burn residue before using them. I taught my brothers to do the same. I learned to hide my single-speaker radio before going to school. I taught my brothers to do the same. I learned to play in the dark when the electricity was cut off. I learned that people were more than comfortable calling my mother "crack head" in front of our young eyes and ears. I learned to grow numb, and I taught my brothers to do the same. The greatest lesson I learned was not to be ashamed of my mother. Trust me when I say that this was no easy task during a time when life was polarized by dichotomies of "clean" or "dirty," "crack head" or human.

These lessons sustained our sanity. These lessons fortified me, along with millions of Black and Latinx families in the 1980s and '90s who too tried to survive life under the "rock."

Being the oldest child, I was charged with ensuring that my brothers were fed and taken care of. While I resented the responsibility, it provided me with a kind of access to my mother that my brothers didn't have. After coming down from her high, she would wake me from my sleep to play board games with her at 2 a.m. She would tell me about how AIDS had stolen her friends and how badly she missed them. She would tell me that I was the "good" one and it was my responsibility to keep my younger brother Nicholas out of trouble. We talked about pretty much everything—except life under the "rock."

It was difficult for anyone in my neighborhood to call someone else's mother a "crack head" without quickly being reminded that their mother too was a "crack head." So the insults had to be more specific; hairs had to be split: "Well at least my mother didn't sell the TV." "Well at least we have food in the house." Life under a rock even impacted how we played the dozens.

My brothers and I were "lucky" in this sense. Our mother had neither sold the TV nor left us without food, and we found solace in that. I believe that this alone helped us to survive with whatever dignity we had left as I watched the will to live disappear from the eyes of other kids living in and being surrounded by crack addiction.

According to the U.S. Sentencing Commission, more than one thousand stories about crack appeared in the press in 1986, with NBC airing over four hundred reports on the crack "epidemic" alone. The media coverage was instrumental in shaping the nation's perception of those who struggled with and/or were directly impacted by crack addiction. This perception has since been inherited by a new generation of HIV advocates and activists, who only associate the presidency of Ronald Reagan with his failed response to AIDS. But those who survived the Reagan years also associate that time with the government's swift and violent response to crack, which stole the lives and promise of many, deliberately destroying Black and brown families.

Over thirty years later, the conversation about addiction has shifted dramatically. The same government that demonized, dehumanized, and then criminalized people like my mother now urges us all to remember that people struggling with addiction have a disease and require love, patience, and treatment. This reminder comes just as the face of addiction is now that of white affluent youth struggling with heroin addiction. This compassion, while critical and necessary, was not made available to Black and brown communities that struggled with the presence of crack. I will venture to say that this approach is still NOT available to individuals who continue to struggle in the shadows of crack addiction.

Yes, it is important that we evolve as a society, and it is equally important that we make amends with ourselves for allowing this to happen on our watch. Even more importantly, we cannot validate our evolution without a true account of what happened, who it happened to, and why it happened in the first place.

I have come a long way from the small room I shared with my mother and brothers. I no longer have to check spoons for burn residue, but I no longer have a family to bear witness to the atrocities we survived.

My mother struggled with addiction until her death. My brother Nicholas was murdered in 2001. I sometimes struggle with survivor's guilt. This is not uncommon for those who have survived war. Every day, I am learning to reconcile my survival with the sacrifices my mother and brother made so that I could live life out from under the "rock."

Nick and Mom.   Nick and me.

Atonement is often the last act of any complete apology. As a nation, how do we atone for the heinous behavior of the government during the Reagan years? It's simple: We don't ignore the heroes of my generation. Instead, we honor the legacies of my mother and every mother who provided light in the darkest days of the war that raged on our families. We memorialize them like we would the heroes who were lost in battle.

The Things Miss Tina Taught Me

LOUIE ORTIZ-FONSECA

IT WAS the late 1980s and the height of my mother's crack addiction. If my memory serves me correctly, it was the height of my entire neighborhood's crack addiction. In many ways, the crack epidemic was the equalizer in our neighborhood. My mother had friends who were lawyers, blue-collar workers, bikers, and business executives—all of them were addicts. I watched them roll in and out of our bedroom "apartment." I never paid them much mind. Probably because if I did, I'd get my ass whipped for being nosy. But it was Tina, my mother's best friend, who always left me mesmerized.

Tina—I called her Miss Tina—was Black, tall, muscular, and unapologetic about her sometimes revealing five-o'clock shadow. She often referred to it as her "daytime" look. I studied her like I should have been studying my math homework. I wanted to identify what it was that made her seem magical, because I wanted it for myself. I wanted to be as fabulous as Miss Tina.

She'd visit my mother at least twice a day. Once after work, when she would show up wearing a hard hat, jeans, and construction boots, and then again later at night, when she'd show up looking like our neighborhood's own Donna Summer. This transformation always inspired me. She was my first tangible proof that we create our own beauty and choose what we become.

I'd ask her questions about her nail color and shoes, but what I really wanted to ask her was how to beat up the boys who called me names. I was too scared to admit that even at eight years old, I was called a "faggot" at school. So my questions were in code. Instead of asking, "How do you deal with people teasing you?" I asked, "How did you get to be so pretty?" Whenever we chatted, however brief the conversation, she made me feel like I was the only person in the world. Tina was God and I was praying at her altar.

One night, I woke up to hear my mom and Tina talking, whispering, and crying. Our apartment, which was just a large room, was divided down the middle by a clothesline and sheets. My brothers and I were in bed on one side and my mother and Tina were on the other side, sitting at the table near the kerosene heater.

"I think you are going to need to go to the hospital," I heard my mother say. I couldn't make out Miss Tina's response, but from what I could gather from the tone, her answer was an adamant refusal. The conversation and the crying continued. I peeked through the sheet and saw Miss Tina's bloodied and swollen face. I wanted to ask what happened, but even then I knew. She got beat up for being herself, just like I got beat up at school. Miss Tina was brave enough to tell someone—my mother. I suppose that should have inspired me to tell my mother about the violence I faced too, but I didn't. I never did.

As I got older, Miss Tina and I developed our own friendship. We'd talk about Janet Jackson, fighting back against homophobes, and AIDS. We talked about the night that she showed up bloody in our room. She told me about the many times she showed up bloody somewhere and found ways of performing her own triage. She told me how she endured. *"Make every fight for your life the fight of your life, honey."* She told me to never do drugs or get AIDS. She made me promise. I promised.

In the late 1980s, that was the only HIV prevention there was to give young gay boys: demands to never get AIDS. While I didn't understand completely what Tina was asking of me, I knew exactly what she was saying. When you are a young gay boy, you look for hints and clues. You learn to read between the lines. This was a language Tina and I spoke.

Miss Tina died of AIDS complications in 1996. She passed away quietly. There was no wailing or explicit mourning. People spoke about her death as a matter of fact. I can't say I blame them. By that time, there were an estimated 23 million people living with HIV worldwide. While advances in HIV treatment had just become available and were all but resurrecting people who had been expected to die, AIDS was still ravaging Black, Latinx, poor, and LGBTQ communities. Trauma and shame meant many of us didn't talk with our families about AIDS and death. During one of the last conversations I remember having with Tina, she shared stories of her friends, so many friends, who had succumbed to AIDS complications and were buried in shame. She painted me a real-life picture that I had only seen in made-for-TV movies and would possibly eventually experience myself.

It has been more than twenty years since Tina's passing. It was only through writing this piece that I remembered the promise I made to her. I didn't keep it. I tried drugs, and I discovered they weren't my thing. I have been living with HIV for more than ten years. If this were 1996, I'd be considered a long-term survivor or a medical miracle.

But Tina wasn't really asking me to promise to abstain. She was telling me to live. Tina knew, even before I had officially "come out" to her, that I was in need of direction and helpful hints that could, and would, eventually save my life. I have never once felt as if I somehow had broken the promise I made. I have lived.

Four decades since the onset of the AIDS epidemic and more than fifteen years after Tina's death, effective treatment and care have helped to make HIV a survivable condition. We now even have PrEP, the daily pill that helps to prevent HIV infection. It all would seem like science fiction to Tina and the little boy she knowingly—and unknowingly—saved. All this living.

Today, I am older than Tina was when she died. I still talk about Janet Jackson, fighting homophobes, and AIDS. I perform my own triage when stigma, shame, and blame leave me wounded. I even, through my advocacy work, have the privilege of providing LGBTQ youth the same direction and guidance Tina once gifted me. I am thriving—that, after all, was the real promise I made to her.

Maria's Song, 1999

ARMANDO ALLEYNE

I visited you
and watch you wither
like an old oak tree

HIV and young
and yet old
as far as the sickness
nestled
in your womb
ssshhh, sssshhh
don't tell me you didn't
use protection
I told you even though
you are positive
you have to protect yourself
there's different viruses, strains
that can bedevil the bones
suck dry the very soul
leaving dust for withered skin

glistening smiles
were your last words
as your body crumbled
in masked coma
heaving plastic
doll-like motion
my poor sister
soul cascading to another
realm
her physical body still

heaving, living mechanically
I watch you crumble

I prayed helplessly
for your light
I watch you leave
and didn't resist
we moaned our sister
like it was, wasn't it
our own reflections
you knowing my gayness
my knowing your positive boyfriend
your light heaving spirit
succumbed
to the sky horizon

I admit I did not know
you, nor recognize you any more
in the darkness
I called your name
only to remember shared secrets and thoughts
we hugged and wrapped
amongst ourselves

Maria's Song (#2)

ARMANDO ALLEYNE

life was so sweet
like a juicy orange
for her
a dark rose
black as the night
sweet as the moon

she cascaded
onward
toward the heavens
an angel
walking upon gods path
her blessed spirit
caressing the air
prancing with wind
and longing to reach
for her boyfriend

horses hooves prancing
in the wind
little Maria
watch the clouds
from heaven
little Maria
a woman
high above
how she bends down
to watch us roam

fly on Maria,
fly on angels wings

Context

The *Maria's Song* Series

THE MARIA'S SONG series is about my sister Maria Alleyne, who had AIDS and also suffered from Kaposi's sarcoma. The way I painted her body is influenced by Édouard Manet's reclining nude Olympia, the painting with the Black child holding a basket of flowers. At the time, I was looking at the way artists such as Romare Bearden and Betye Saar used colors. Unlike in Manet's painting, I chose the beach as the scenery behind my sister, with one exception. In this interior scene she's lying in the midst of all these lockers, a reflection of my life in the shelter as well as hers— floating from SROs to hospitals and back. Maria was a Black Puerto Rican like me. I surrounded her with angels and hieroglyphics. It was my way of letting her spirit go.

I wrote two poems about my sister Maria after her passing. She was a Leo, a very strong and fiery spirit but with a soothing, maternal side. She was a combination of so many things, and I wanted to capture them all in the paintings and the poetry.

A photograph of Maria, my younger sister, at her graduation in the mid-'70s from Seward Park High School in Manhattan. We didn't get along when we were kids, but we outgrew that. In the mid-'90s she told me she was HIV positive; she had these dark spots on her skin at the time. I had promised my father, who was also sick, that I would take care of her. My father died in 1996 and Maria followed in 1999.

The bird-of-paradise flower is said to give life. Above it a skull is hovering—death; the blooming of death and the rapid spread of the disease. I didn't intend to make the *Maria's Song* series something beautiful. My only purpose was to describe the metamorphosis of life into death.

Originally there were six or seven *Maria's Song* paintings, but most of them were damaged while being stored in a brownstone uptown, damaged by mold and mildew when the basement flooded. It was Michael's basement, as I was living at the shelter at the time. I was still doing artwork in the shelter, but most of it was taken because it was considered a fire hazard underneath the mattress or behind the locker. This led me to be more and more aloof, more isolated and depressed. I'm not sure whether or not I ever understood what was going on because I felt like the system was controlling me.

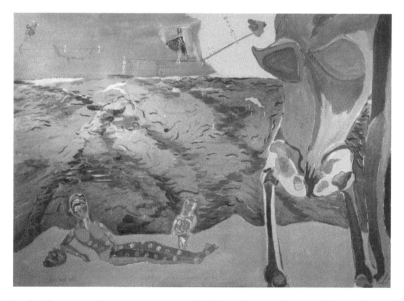

In the '90s era there were several things happening, and people would get these dark spots on their skin from AIDS. I didn't know how to paint them on my sister's body, so I made designs, some with eyes representing the third eye. I used to think that the eyes are the soul. I was trying to deal with death and its symbols. My father had just passed and my sister was dying. I still miss visiting her every couple of days.

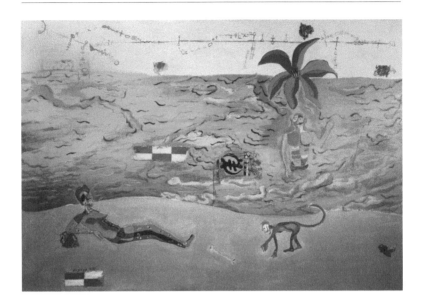

The symbolism of the monkey is lucky and happy, but I painted this one with the face of a skull. To me, this series is about re-creation and metamorphosis. I used to work on individual paintings all at the same time. I usually work like this, simultaneously. I also dedicated artwork to my other sister Yolanda, who later passed of breast cancer. The piece *The Lasky Family* from 1999 shows her with her son and husband with a building in the background—my rendition of my tenement building versus her projects.

Polluted Imprints in a Neurodivergent Mind

JULIA FELIZ

A S SOCIETY insists on pressing me for answers about truths lost long ago that the modern world's majority cannot imagine or understand, I find myself responding easily, "I have none."

Internally, my mind instinctively begins to self-soothe: "Your outward appearance doesn't define you. You know yourself, where you came from, where you have been, how it made you feel, and how you validated yourself when no one even knew you needed validation, not even you. Your existence is ancestral survival. It is resistance." To me, this is the familiar slipping of consciousness that leads to the comforts of my inattentive neurodivergence . . .

Within the safe space of my mind, I can feel myself uninhibitedly scanning endlessly for glimpses of what constitutes my story. I find myself trying to recall the moment I felt safe enough to tell the world my truth. That moment exists, but at the same time, it does not exist. This is because the thought leads me to memories that were forced on me—by others.

I distinctly say "forced" because I have never consented to the expectations or the assumptions that have followed me even as I tried to shed them rigorously after I realized they were not mine and never had been.

None of the memories I have which are tied to my identity are mine.

Despite not being mine, the memories I do have undoubtedly shaped much of who I was, who I hid, who I have become, and who I had to hide again for my own protection. The world, including those closest to me, is not ready to accept those like me—erased despite forming an accepted part of the communities whose blood survives within my veins. The memories carried in me are those shaped by a violent history that was forced on my ancestors and subsequently stole my ability and right to exist safely. This history, my history, is one that has compartmentalized me, and those like me, for over 520 years. The memories I hold have been built upon a self that has been divided piece by piece according to the by-products of that history through erasure, homophobia, transphobia, binarism, anti-Blackness, anti-Indigeneity, colorism, classism . . . They are polluted imprints programmed within my mind's eyes from the moment I took my first breath and was tagged with an assigned gender at birth. These memories are recollections of a conscious and subconscious journey that has hindered, denied, and diluted my identity, breaking it into pieces that are not allowed to exist together.

In contrast, when I allow myself to think specifically about my authentic self, I easily sense a deeply sown, unnamed sentiment that comforts me. This "sentiment" has always been part of my essence. It has always been there, steadily protected, shielded from the denial of my being and the binary expectations that I have never named as my own, like the memories of the person who I am assumed to be. This part of me, however, has always been an accepted constant—a component of what makes me who I am, which I have known as intrinsically me across my childhood and adolescence, and throughout my adulthood. In my soul, I feel it is the acknowledgment of a truth within me that no one else but me has been able to touch, taste, hear, see, and smell.

While society undoubtedly taught me to mimic its expectations under the threat of punishment should I veer off my predesignated gendered path, I have always been the feelings that only I have known. Within my own skin, I simply exist, comfortably and at peace. This is my essence, unspoiled by whiteness's insistence on who and what I am.

Ocean Home

ZOË GAMELL BROWN

My ancestors are from the water
I feel them in my fingers
When I walk
Along the cold coast
I smell my mother's hair
Musky and maternal
As the ocean air
Now I know why
I feel at ease
When I take deep breaths
While I sit by the sea
And hear the ocean say,
"Don't go away
don't fret, don't fear.
You're supposed to be here."

Of Joy (A Bricolage)

RANDY JAMES

From Río Abajo & the archipelago come *mamá*,
her sisters, daughters & sons—their children.
On their tongues, English comes seasoned, finely pickled.
"Shrimp" becomes *strimp*
through *mamá*'s Poligrip dentures.
"Little" 'comes *likkle* when
my mother's in a jaunty mood.
What happened? becomes *wha'ppen*
in my youngest uncle's mouth.
If it's been a long time, my eldest aunt will ask me, *¿Qué pasó, cara chicle?*
In their mouths, my name grows limbs, becomes
a one-word tale in the lilt of my favorite aunt.

My daddy's Alabaman tongue crops spontaneous: there, where my
words soft their edges.
Like, sometimes potato becomes *'tato.*
What happened? becomes *wha'appened?*
Maybe, too, in his "yeahhh buddy," maybe mine, maybe us concerted,
flipping off the eyes.
In my daddy's country tongue, kid me ain't kid me at all, but *Doodoo-bug* & *Pootytat.*
His tongue's not all cotton, though—sometimes
it's tender crispy, AM dials & rented books,
a Corona beer at the end of rein-y workdays.
In my father's speech, well-oiled Toyota Tercels
get names like Judy, last names like Blue.

Ancestor in Barbados

RANDY JAMES

No human sound,
in Crop Over
they snatch their own
whoops & hollers

Shak-shak & banjo
triangle & bones
fiddle & guitar—
they speak in stead

The tears that burn
his cheeks the clink
of earthen jars
to get around
the chain

He sees the love
left behind
in the twist of
the dancing girl's
hips the sweet center
of the circle's
secret relief

Feels free

On This Little Island

RANDY JAMES
after Richard Ligon

I.

We ape sympathy & sentiment on the back of Sunday dancers. Our
balls light up pineapples & palm trees. Craning their necks in gales of
laughter to strains of theorbo
& divers kettle drums, our finest are fine cream, fine tan, fine red. They
dress in green taffeta striped with white & philiamort. Our free ones
wear silver badges round
the small of their legs—temper English spirits in the round of a
calabash—
wait on the display of white teeth.

II.

O u r   m u s k e t s   a r e
t a l k i n g   d r u m s
t o   q u e l l   d a r k   r e b e l l i o n s

III.

They (by the laws of England)
cannot be Christian & made to toil
in the same manner.
They (without letters or numbers)
reckon by the moon.
Some (like Sambo)
are allowed an ear
upon His door but nothing
of the blood.

IV.

In the communion of our planters
 in the glow of sugar-make
  we share best remedies:

Lyam hounds for Maroons / Palm-oil
for the outside—kill-devil
for the in / Severed heads
on dozen high poles
for suicide courtiers
to kill notions of return
to their own countries
on this little island.

V.

Forsake the God that moves the clouds
& blooms at our feet—
the God that gave us boilers
for the sugar-make?
To go back on this would be remiss.

Ode to Abuela

RAQUELLE MAYORAL

I honor you with Bustelo on a silver platter
and a piece of bread from la panadería,
like the one five houses down the street
around the corner and to the right of your pink house.

I'd like to imagine the bakery still stands.
I'd like to imagine Maria didn't take it . . .
                        the hurricane didn't take you.
Imagine the heartbreak of seven years without your beloved
or if the cancer hadn't spread.

I imagine your smile wider than the coastal view
we see atop Titi's stone oasis. Your teeth are
treasured pearls found along the shore.
Your laughter, drizzled honey en pan.
Skin like fresh coffee-sugar-and a drop of milk.

I imagine you at your brightest.
Hanging wash in the backyard, full of hibiscus
and chickens searching dirt for food.
The air thick with humidity and Fania.
The sun, a torch amid palmas.

How is it where you are?

[Untitled]

FRANCHESCA ARAÚJO

I see the world [   ] hands
[   ] hands won't tell me anything
It seems too painful

I see decades of trespassed body ownership in [   ] hands
I see a woman I'll never know through her own stories
[   ] wrote about what it means to come from an island,
surrounded by Ocean, surrounded by no more than one other
nation-state
What (that) does to your thinking
The ocean swallows islanders up and takes away what is possible, quite
different from the sanctity of endless water we usually hear in poetry,
In prose,
In stories of Santos

I wonder if the ocean swallowed [   ] up
Her healing and sense of deserving
Her courage to talk
Her ability to comfort her daughters

It's too painful to read books about Balaguer, about sex tourism, little
girls on the beach

I was raised on a continent
There is more than water around me
There is more than one border
I think about the little girls all of the time

I hope I inherited [   ] thoughts too, on the trip across the
ocean that swallowed her up.

I hope the little she says
The absence of what she tells
Means she's holding nothing

The plant speaks for the girl buried under it / O lixo fala pela menina enterrada debaixo dele (with glimmers of Clifton)

FRANCHESCA ARAÚJO

To listen, walk, feet bare on soil

When you hear faint echoes, whispers
Stop

To listen, caress with bare hands

It wants to speak for those it remembers

Many **Bakhitas**, undocumented, unfound

She is 20 years old
She is from Guinea

She is five foot four

She remembers her mother

She is relieved that Oyá found her earlier instead of later,

Even after crossing miles of blue to another world
"Good news about the earth!": the plant speaks for the girl under it

And "being property once herself"
She "has a feeling for it"
That's why she can talk through "what wants to be a tree"

She is given a better homegoing, the one that is owed, and was stolen
When I listen

She is given a proper homegoing,
When?

Remembering

REVA SANTO

8.8.19

6:30 A.M. and the city buzzes with energy. Kids hustle off to school, workers run to catch the bus. Mothers walk, balancing babies on their hips, dragging another along by hand. Tiny feet bounce along the concrete. A bus turns down a small sun-kissed street. A man pushes a cart past a plant shop. Another walks his daughter to school. A third buys coffee off the side of the road. A siren goes off—a cop car appears from behind and clears through the traffic. It's the first time I've been in Salvador, Bahia, with my dad since I was thirteen, and five and a half years since my last visit.

I ask Dad if the memories flood him when he visits. He says they do. Yesterday we ran around town gathering things to prepare an offering for Xangô, starting first at a small alley-like street filled with fruit and vegetable vendors and lined with shops selling Candomblé goods. My cousin Matteus* received the family trait de poder receber Santo. His mom, my Tia Nila*, receives the spirit of an ancestor, M*. I'm not exactly sure who M* is, though I've talked to her many times.

Dad says that everyone here is in survival mode. He has a lot of memories associated with this place. A distant home. Working at the feira São

---

1. Excerpts from this piece were first used in Reva Santo's short film *remembering* (2020), a visual meditation on diaspora, family, and life cycles composed through collaged words, photographs, videos, and performances.

Joaquim selling fruits at thirteen. The pink house where Mestre Valdemar lived. The yellow-tiled spot on the corner where he first saw capoeira. Dad tells me of his dreams of creating a community center in Liberdade, in the small house that held four generations, now five, of our family.

My great-grandfather Ciriaco was Portuguese. According to my Tia Nila*, he abandoned my great-grandmother Maria Isidoria after having six children with her. He was white, she was Black, and his family didn't approve. He left us the land, though. Tia Nila* says to ask my vovó the whole story, she's the family historian, she'll know everything that happened. Nila* is the daughter of my grandmother's sister, who passed last year. My vovó is the last one of her siblings still alive, and she carries all of the stories with her.

Memories emerge of M*, lighting a cigar by stove top, sipping her cerveja from a glass, hand on her hip. "Você gostou de mim?" she asked matter-of-factly, after having told me much of my family history and advised me about personal life matters. I was nineteen at the time, and unsure of everything, wary of the magic and depth in my family lineage, but just as much intrigued. Older now, I feel myself gaining a better understanding of it all. Somehow only now do I understand the energy that exists in this particular plot of land. And I wonder if it is because Tia Nila* lives on our ancestral land that she was gifted this connection to M*. Must be. Must be why my primo Matteus* receives Xangô and another ancestor. I ask Dad if M* is an ancestor and he says yes, and I wonder from when. He tells me that our lineage is strong. This time around I can feel what that means, and I'm no longer afraid of it.

In the car on the way to Guarajuba today, words were floating in the air and I tried to grasp them with my weak, jet-lagged hands. The TV turns off and I feel the grip around my brain loosen. I can hear the waves again. My family shows love through physical affection. Rubbing my back, taking the time to fix up all the ends of my braids. Preparing food. Affectionately holding a wrist. Nonverbal communication goes far. Perhaps they see my tenderness, though in this half-sleep state I am often unwilling to talk. I want(ed) to speak with all of the Egun today. All of the ancestors that I have perhaps forgotten by mistake. I want the names I never knew to arrive on my tongue as if I had always known them. I want to hear all of their secret messages. Vovó knows all the stories but sometimes I grow tired just trying to absorb them all. It's going to take time for me to really understand the purpose of this trip. I'm not sure what home is. But I know this land is loaded with history. The chaos of so many people and all of their ancestors. This land seems to carry energy with a force.

8.9.19

Today is rainy. I felt hesitant to do yoga on the balcony, because I didn't want the men outside to look at me, but I realized pretty quickly, everyone is just living their own lives. The man who cuts hair is across the street in the same spot he has always been. I remember when he was a teenager. I was a baby. Now he's in his forties with a potbelly hanging over his shorts. In that same place. The water rushes toward the shore pressured by the pounding rain. I look out at the docks and see a few figures standing. Everything here moves in a circle. Little girls learn the vocabulary to become women. They become teenagers walking with pride and a calm security. They learn early on how to ignore the persistent "sssssss" of older men. Soon a baby will be balanced on that hip or she'll hustle off in a uniform to work a blue-collar or corporate job. At home the novelas await. The sisters wait. The food waits. The husband, boyfriend, daddy may or may not be there.

Little boys run around with their sisters until they are old enough to pick up soccer balls, or old enough to gather and tell jokes huddled around the bench. I don't know when exactly the boys and the girls start falling in love. All I know is I left and my younger cousin was seven, drawing in her little notebook. Now she's thirteen and knows just how to ignore the men who look at her as she walks the streets with her friends. All I know is I left and my younger cousin was ten, and now he's sixteen, been in love once, has an ex-girlfriend who likes to talk my ear off about winning him back. Now he listens to music on his headphones and complains when his mom asks him to do something. The other night, walking with my cousin Lady just to get some air, we pass a familiar face. A young teenager whistles at me. I know that face, his mother maybe eight years older than me, knew me when I was young. I can see her face imprinted on his. I remember when she was pregnant. I remember approaching her house asking if she knew a place to get chocolate. I remember her asking my cousin se eu estava grávida. I remember saying yes, not knowing at the time that "grávida" meant pregnant. My cousin laughing at my error. All I know is her baby boy is old enough to know these social codes, how men are meant to look at women.

I don't know when exactly the boys and girls start falling in love, I only see when the babies come. Some of them will hustle with gangs. I do not fully know that world. Only a boy who tried to kiss me once, who showed me a bandage and said he got stabbed in a fight. Only an older cousin who was shot in his sleep when I was too young to understand what death meant. Only an ex-lover who puffed out his chest and created a force field around me on a late Saturday night in Liberdade when two men began to argue. The rest I've only heard in stories. Other men and women too will begin pushing carts, gathering car parts, selling coffee and cerveja, bringing fish to grandmothers. They come home to food and dominoes. They come home to beer and brothers. At a certain age they will all retire perhaps, when their kids are old enough. They will just play dominoes, or they will just watch TV. They will just yell orders or jokes at grandkids as the next generation rises, watching, learning, repeating.

But what of the renegades? What of the queers and the sex workers and the rebels? What of the political activists and the nerds and the failures? Where in the cycle are they? Do they survive underground? Do they survive? Are they pushed out of the circle to exist in loose orbit? Not entirely out of the flow, but most certainly not within it. Where are they hiding and what did their families think when they left? Who would I be if I had been born here? How would I have conformed or disrupted? How would I have pleased or disappointed? How would I have chosen to survive?

8.10.19

I come in and my auntie tells me I shouldn't tie up my hair with a black elastic. I also shouldn't use my own hair to make a ponytail. There are so many superstitions, I wonder where they originate from.

The family is preparing a barbecue today. Dad and I slipped away in the early morning to speak with my ancestor M*. She had a lot to say about my romantic life and my willingness (or lack thereof) to fight for what/whom I really want. She spent a lot of time trying to explain to me that it's important for me to know how to prepare limpezas for myself. I need to know how to protect myself, she says. I can't come home and just sit in the negativity from the world. I can't wait around for others to help me, I should really listen and learn how to do it on my own. I feel like this is the piece I was missing last time. The piece to all of the magic. The ability to protect myself from the negativity that inevitably exists in the world. The ability to heal myself and clear my own path. There's something of resilience here that whispers to me of ancestral survival. This is how my people were able to live through the years of slavery on this land. It is magic that we have survived. I am honored to inherit this tradition which has enabled my existence.

This may be the last time I ever visit my family in this way. Not to be malicious. Just an observation. The queer in me is just begging to burst out. There's not much space for any of that here. I wonder which spirits are listening to me when I speak in silence.

Dad's outside with my vovó and the capoeiristas. I think she's sad that he's leaving because she wants everyone to always be together. There is a different kind of responsibility and obligation that comes when I return to this house. It's the family structure, everyone rolls together, everyone stays here, returns here. I know I needed to come here for ancestral reasons. I'm not at all doubting that. Just feeling like a bit of an outsider, but trying to lean into it.

Growing up, my older cousin was always trying to convince me to get with some boy. I always trusted her judgment, and now I look back at all the people and know that perhaps I shouldn't have. So me now, older, wiser . . . What of her now? My beloved cousin. What of all the thoughts and feelings undigested that lived in the pit of my stomach, or the roots of my hair? This hair has not yet breathed the air of this country. Almost all of my cells have regenerated in the time span that I have been gone, but there are just enough left to remember.

It's hot, sticky, and itchy. I am uncomfortable, but growing. Uncomfortable, but good. Sinking deeper always. Vision growing clearer always. Heart becoming purer always. And even if my skin grows rashes and my hair falls out, there will always be fresh skin waiting to break through the surface and breathe new air.

8.11.19

I told my cousin I was queer yesterday, dropped an ex-partner casually in conversation. Today she reads a book with the subtitle "How to Save Someone You Love." I just laugh. She keeps asking me if I'm okay, but I can tell she's the one who is uncomfortable. I wish she'd just ask me the questions she has.

It's basically a family reunion here today. Aunties, uncles, cousins, new babies all pouring out the walls at this point. Social anxiety on ten today. I only know how to stand behind the camera and take photos. To be in the picture is a different thing.

My family is professional at surface conversations. *How's your mom? How's your brother? Have you eaten?* Everyone likes to gossip about what other people are doing. Yesterday my tia Jaci was talking about some neighbor friend and how she got cheated on by her boyfriend with her friend. My cousin was scandalized. My auntie was explaining that she had screenshots of the conversations and offered to show them to my cousin. I'm honestly just bored by it. It's frustrating. I have absolutely no interest in hearing the judgmental drama of other folks. And yet here I am judging them for doing it.

5:08 P.M.

Not even a full week has passed. I am here at the airport dropping off Dad. Today, more of the family poured in to visit. To say bye to Dad, to eat a meal for Dia dos Pais. I feel like a comfortable outsider. I've enjoyed having my dad close. He understands me. He can see when I'm feeling sensitive and he lets me be, makes sure that I'm okay. He speaks to me in English, it becomes our secret language among the family if we need to talk about orixas or Candomblé or things that make my tia Jaci uncomfortable.

We went to visit my tio Gil at the hospital before leaving. I didn't know that his full name was Genilson, but I saw it posted there beside his bed. I didn't expect him to look so sick, so old. In a full room with four other sickly men, half-asleep, emaciated and ill. At the hospital for alcoolismo e acolhimento. I felt overcome with the desire to cry but knew that I had to keep a happy face for him and the others. My tia Jaci and Jeane were in full nurse mode. Checking his body, looking for swelling, Jaci asked him if he knew who she was, if he knew who my dad was, my auntie, and then me.

What, do you think I'm crazy? he said to her and we all laughed.

Aisha, he said. Recognizing me by my middle name.

I'm not sure what really is wrong with him. The health system here is so bad he spent years on a walker and now he's been in the hospital for months; it's hard to see how he can get better. He looks older than my vovó. She's eighty-four, I think he's only sixty. But my auntie insists that he's getting better, which may be true. *We have to keep faith*, she says. *You'll see, next time you visit he'll be back home.* There is an evangelical program on the small TV by the doorway. A girl weeps and a host reminds her to have faith in god.

The skinniest man in the room is curled up, his eyes bulging—he looks at me and lifts his hand slowly. He's saying hello; I smile. I can feel him staring at me as I try to focus on my uncle. Shifting my eye contact as my uncle downloads the information. *How old is she now?* he asks. *Twenty-five,* I say. He seems shocked. Confused maybe. I can't tell if he's unsure about time, but it's clear that I am a woman now. Maybe he's remembering me as a baby. Little Reva Aisha running around in polka-dot onesies refusing to let my mom fix my hair.

It's time for us to leave now, I can tell that Dad is overwhelmed, perhaps slightly anxious to leave. I take my uncle's hand. *Bença meu, tio,* I say. He is too absent to give me his blessing. My dad rubs Tio's head and assures him that next time we see each other it will be at home. For Christmas. *Que vamos passar o natal todo mundo juntos em casa.* My dad kisses my tio's head multiple times. I can tell he's sad to leave. I can tell that despite what he says, he's unsure if he'll ever see his brother again. You can never be sure. You can never be sure. *Eu te amo,* he says. And my uncle, lips quivering, mutters back, *Eu te amo.* I can tell he means it. I can see they both mean it. The love is profound, and the miles and oceans between us are deep. The love is profound and the differences between us are deep.

This is what diaspora does: it liberates and it uproots all at the same time. We are connected only through love. Through these tiny moments, memories that we hold on to, of times when we were all together, hope for future moments when once again we will share the same air and come together to eat food, to laugh, to smile, to be family.

As soon as we leave Tio's room I begin to weep. I thought I could hold it all in, I always do. My tia Jaci is across the hall and she sees me. I approach her as I try to hold in my tears. She drapes her arm around me as we walk out of the hospital. *It's difficult, I know,* she says, *but we have to have faith. He's getting better. You should have seen him before.* She keeps saying affirmations and I'm crying anyways. Overwhelmed and humbled by the tenderness between my dad and his brother, by the care with which my aunties adjusted his bed, made sure he was warm, smiled big and asked questions.

In the car Dad asks me if I'm okay and I begin to cry again. I can't even respond with words. Too overwhelmed to explain what it is that I'm feeling. My auntie reassures me. Rubbing my knee with her hands. I let the tears fall and feel humbled.

It's not that I'm sad that my uncle might be dying. I'm sad that my uncle is in pain. That my uncle can't remember. That my dad has to leave for the airport. That I don't even know my uncle very well. That we all have to live so far apart. That everything is different. That my family will never understand me. I'm sad that so many people in this country feel so hopeless, that institutions take advantage of them. I'm sad that my people are dying for lack of health care. I'm sad that my other people are dying for lack of understanding.

I am humbled because even with all of the miles and all of the differences, we are here loving each other. My evangelical auntie and my Candomblé father. My queer radical self and my conservative cousin. My judgmental, caring, rambunctious grandmother and my thoughtful, sarcastic, disabled auntie. All of us. We are all wearing the faces of our ancestors. We are walking the paths that feel most authentic to each of us. We are all navigating fear and confronting it the best we can. Even as we continue misunderstanding one another and judging one another. Somehow, still, we are able to love. That to me is beyond words. And for that, I wept.

A pregnant teenager walks by in a miniskirt. My dad comments that every young girl here is pregnant, and everyone in the car agrees. I'm twenty-five now and it's true. A lot of the girls I knew have disappeared into their homes, become moms, grown bellies. They stay in the house now. Mothers younger than me. My tia Jaci comments on the way they dress, as if they were asking to be fucked and impregnated. It's not their fault, I think to myself. It's this whole world. Wearing a longer skirt has nothing to do with it. It has to do with shitty education, boredom, and culture teaching girls that the only thing that matters is their appearance and attention from men. It's not their fault, I think. But I stay quiet.

And still . . .

The duality of this place is this.

Today I finally make it to FUNCEB to take an Afro-contemporary dance class and see a friend from college who lives here now. She tells me that she was feeling called to uncover her roots, to learn more about the Candomblé and the Lucumí in her heritage. To dance, learn music, connect.

The energy in class is high. Somehow in the five and a half years since I've been here, I've forgotten that the connection is profound. This is the reason I'm here. For these moments when the drums beat so close to my heart I can close my eyes and trust them to carry me. Sweat pours onto the ground as we dance for the orixas. I can feel ancestors filling the space around me. This is a safe haven, perhaps, for all those unsettled spirits who never elevated, who stay lurking around the historic colonial district of Pelourinho. Here, we dance, we honor, we remember.

After class I am ten tons lighter. My spirit is high. My friend and I grab a beer and spend a couple of hours talking about the experiences we've had, the high ancestral energy here, how important it feels to be back, even as we navigate the privilege of U.S. citizenship, the privilege of the strength of our USD versus Brazilian reais. Even as we navigate the feelings of isolation that come with it.

I get home and write this down:

I will use my body to connect my spirit

to the sky.
I will use my body, I will use my body.
I will become a portal for light.
I will be strong, despite inevitable shadow.
I am unafraid.

The drums beat and I feel the feet
of my ancestors pounding this Earth
below me.

We are together,
have always been, even if I forget
from time to time.
We are united by breath and blood
and unseen energy.
Connected by sound and breath and
movement we are together always.

I broke through, I continue breaking.
My body still carries dead weight
but it burns away slowly, surely.

Truth guides my heart and my tongue.
Patience at the back of my throat
and I know that there are really beautiful
surprising, profound,
joyous
moments coming my way.

I feel it in my bones
mixed in among the sadness
(when it comes),

the sweet nostalgia
of past love.
I am in love, I am in love.
I am always in love
with life, with this land,
with the way the wind moves
with the way the water and the sky meet
in tenderness.

8.13.19

I'm sitting here and I do not know what to tell you. I do not know what to tell you. I do not know how to speak of this place, of the experiences. Of the division in my body from base to skull. Of the full split, left from right. I am divided. I am trying to find comfort and truth, but today I am just tired. I'll leave my house to get the candles, to buy snacks, to sit by the ocean, to hear the music.

The words will come again.

Where Is Home?

IVANOVA VERAS DE JESÚS

The sun is right . . . on my face,
The dirt is right on my face,
I close my eyes,
We need to rest.

With my eyes closed,
I see Mamá, my grandma,
I see her heavy,
The weight of the world
lands on her . . . back.

The colonizers say she was born dirty,
She never forgets,
She's never allowed to,
They don't get the majesty of her Black skin.

I smell the sweat running down her neck, *my* neck?
I feel her calluses on my feet,
Her cloudy hands are my own,
My lips form an "o,"
And her whistle comes out,
Guiding the wind,
Making trees grow,
Directing the rain.
Our knees are hurting,
And so are our souls.
I wonder:
Who were you
before they told you who to be?
Which parts of you are missing?

What dreams were deemed too big?
How often was love denied to you?
How are you standing?
Where are we anyway?
Why I hear a voice telling me I don't belong? Is that their voice?
Why is it inside me?
Did I swallow it?
How do I shut it out?

Mamá, Mamita, mi sol,
Where is Home?
How did we get here?
Why do my roots hurt?
Do I really die if I cut them off?
What exact amount of strength have we built? How are we still
standing?

With my eyes still closed,
>   I am reunited with Mamá,
>   And her grandparents,
>   And their grandparents,
>   And their grandparents.
>   I recognize every face,
>   Every step,
>   I feel every river,
>   Inside of me,
>   Where they belong,
>   Home.

my gram's machete

JR MAHUNG

MY GRAM'S machete long. a black-handled thing. blade bleak with rust but still wave n break a blade of grass, crack a coconut, peel a plantain, chop a tree stump in the backyard, will *chop yo dutty hands if you no leave my kitchen bwai heck!* my gram's machete steady to the left, right & front. will sign a cross & beckon the archangel. *be our protection against the wickedness.* my gram's machete a cutlass in trinidad, a smile on our south side porch. stands at attention in uniform—house dress over sweatpants & hoodie. sandals on the feet. my gram's machete not made for this cold *not at all my boy.* gets real harsh when it snows, keeps to its room. remembers heat like dangriga. a knock at the window can shake my gram's machete. but believe it's still steady & prepared to cut. can put itself at ease too. jehovah's witness, a copy of the watchtower in tow. gram's machete say: here. a place the lord's children are welcome but cannot stay. *jehovah understand.* my gram's machete stay near the front door, in the kitchen closet by the back, under the bed, next to the wray & nephew.

letter to simone
(on the subject of the king)

JR MAHUNG

most of what i know is imagined
chatoyer was born & then he lived
& then he didn't. his hands perhaps looked
something like my uncle's, calloused palms,
fingers thick. *he was not a violent man*
at least i like to think, though he did fight
& he did kill. i suppose you know
better than me, the ways a life can be an impossible demand how
death can stare from the end of it. do you ever dream of the ones who
lived so you could live after? is it different from remembering?

letter to simone
(on cutting grass)

JR MAHUNG

you said yourself
we're headed for the brink & i think
perhaps we've been there. my dad
says back home they used machete
to cut grass, cut weeds, cut vines.
                    there's more he didn't say but
must be true still. the grass grows
back the weeds return to choke it
& vines they climb & climb &
climb
we can't forget that, no

reflections on watching
missy elliott's "lose control" video

JR MAHUNG

my gram hums & i imagine a chorus
behind her we listen to paul nabor. she
tells me "when i die, bury me with music."
a man on youtube said "it is your duty to
care for this land until we can return."
there was a time before the music.
garinagu before us with a whole world to
build. a professor this morning says we
came from a king. that our name means
those who traded in gold.

consider another tale, a people who tasted
cassava & called ourselves after that dark root
which kept us. consider our beginning an
unburied body *everybody   everybody
here* is where imagination lives   *everybody
                                    get loose*

portrait of my grandmother in 90s hip-hop videos

JR MAHUNG

wu-tang ain't nuthin ta fuck wit

fire & explosion at the beginning
inspectah deck opens the chorus.
everyone is in their hoodies & ski masks
gram steps out wearing her black hat,
& a jacket over a hoodie over her nightgown
over a pair of sweatpants. she is holding her machete
gram scolds the wu-tang clan says "cho! who make that
noise? you boys grown & no know how to act? want to
blow up the whole building what is that? using those foul
words in your mouth it late & it cold for this now too!"
gram becomes more fervent, she shakes her machete at the
wu-tang clan,

"you boys go from here before i beat every jack one of
you" the gza, the rza, ol dirty bastard, method man,
ghostface, inspectah deck, raekwon, u-god, & masta killa
run home promptly everyone makes it home in time for
supper. the video ends with gram sitting comfortably in her
big chair watching the "days of our lives" as she eats tortilla
with stewed chicken feet

beep beep
who got the keys to the jeep?

missy pulls up in a black hummer
says she is going to the beach but stops short
before vroom. gram raises her hand from her front porch

and yells "gyal heck! you go leave without me chuh!"
gram ambles to the passenger seat in her big black coat
which she's got over her nightgown
draped over a hoodie & sweatpants

"your cousin syl call
& ask for powder bun take me to jewel
we need margarine"
as it turns out gram also needed to buy a calling card,
find cassava, pick up her prescriptions, & get her lotto numbers missy
never makes it to the beach

juicy

gram walks into biggie's mansion wearing her big coat
over a hoodie over her nightgown over a pair of sweatpants
everyone is partying by the pool. when she realizes there
are no slots, gram says "oh no. this no the casino"

i left my wallet in el segundo

the video is almost entirely the same up until q-tip
mentions he ordered enchiladas & he ate em while ali
shaheed muhammad only had a fruit punch. the visual cuts to
gram in her jacket over a hoodie over her nightgown which
she is wearing over a pair of sweatpants. she is cooking rice & beans, says
"you drive that far & get food & this boy have what!?! juice?!? what kinda
thing that? you eat & let your friend starve? that is not the way boy cho!
el
segundo & no food?!! ayyyyy jesus!" gram heaps a small
mountain of rice on a plate for ali. he begins to say he's not
hungry but gram cuts him off "shush boy eat" before
addressing q-tip "now go to the store & get me coconut
milk. i use it all
on this boy rice." tip reminds gram he doesn't have his wallet
gram replies "that your problem not mine. go get my milk"

four page letter

aaliyah emerges from the forest path
begins climbing up a fallen tree trunk
gram's voice enters "gyal you gon fall from
there & bust up your head chuh! in your good
leather outfit too. leave that damn boy alone gyal
here" embarrassed, aaliyah walks back to the path.
aaliyah & gram find a bench to sit & pen a letter
to the jehovah's witnesses down the street instead
asking that they please leave the house alone

¿Y Vos Quién Sos?

CLARA OLIVO

My identity is my deepest secret
A mystery slowly unraveled by time
Desperation for belonging
Free from isolation and shame
Bound by centuries of falsehood
Deflection
Erasure

Latinidad told me that there are no Black people in El Salvador
That "colocha" is something to taunt
A slur
Had I been born with my father's hair
Would I be more lost?
Wandering in the fog
Looking for the light
That will make me divine
Make me loved?
Or would I be in community?
Unafraid to profess my love for my dark skin
For the colochos that bounce as I walk this madre earth
Unapologetic and free
Certain of who I am because I "look the part"
I *feel* it

But what does it even mean
To "look" Salvadoreña?
Society invalidates me
My people
My country

My country invalidates me
My roots
My history
Erased

They say that there are no Black people in El Salvador
Look closely, look farther
Back . . .
Back . . .
It's in our history
In our blood
In my skin
In my heart

Though I am my mother's daughter
I too am my father's child
A legacy I struggle to know
Embracing
El Negro y Su Negrita
A forbidden love denied
Rejected
Abandonada cuando lo más amaba
A lifeline to my past
My history
My roots
Lost
When he walked away

Clarita Escucha Su Voz

CLARA OLIVO

The times I want to call you
(are) When the nostalgia hits
The need for tender love and care
that only a father could bring
I stop in my tracks
Think back . . .   back . . .   back . . .
When pre-K Clara needed you to pick her up after school (because
mama was working late, cleaning her 4th house of the day in the beau-
tiful Hollywood hills)
When 8-year-old Lala lost her big sister (her best friend)
¿Y dónde estabas?
Espera, no importa

You never stepped up or *in* the times that it mattered
So why should I?

Oh . . .

There was that one time
One time
When Clara in her early 20s flew from houston to l.a.
The day after mama passed away
I don't remember how she got your number
but I do remember saying
"Mama is gone . . . se murió"
The static crackling through the words
You made me repeat them
despite the interference and bad reception
My words became your new reality
Loud and clear

You said you would come
Crossing mountains and highways to be there for me
And mira no más, there you were
Ready to receive me in your arms
Pressing all the pain and disbelief out of me

That TLC I know only a dad can bring
That moment of stillness, of relief
I knew it wouldn't last
Because the day of the funeral, you said you would be there
And for a moment I believed it

Until

Pre-K Clara tugged at my arm
Reminding me that she's still waiting to get picked up

          And 8-year-old Clara
Reminds me that you can't show your sadness and you gotta be strong
         And just like that
We put down the phone

[7 December 2020]

untitled

DES JACKSON

I wander, I wonder
these lost and dark waters—my soul
—my mind
I'm behind
help me find . . .

I wonder where I lost myself
and where I went
I wonder what I was looking for
and if I wandered off into the abyss

the old me, that's who I miss

staring at the same 4 walls
categorized and caged in
check the box and there you have it
Bona Fide Human
is it possible to ever just Be?
to exist just to breathe and to see?

I yearn for a life without time, without limits
without the lens I see through-and-in, it
is a world which contains all I want to call home
where the sand laces between my toes and
the wind whispers in my ear to soothe my woes

and is it possible to live without this desire?

so deep and so steep and the reaper chases close behind;
Is it possible to be satisfied?

imagine no hunger or need of a feast
to eternally be at ease and appeased—
how cursed are we by our obligations, aren't we

to
Be

Un Cuento del Regreso

JEHOIADA ZECHARIAH CALVIN

When I was a child,
Mamá told me that

one day, they were able to finally see
that the answer they had been searching for
had never left them to begin with.

And the story goes that

those who jumped and knew to swim
went to the core of the Earth.

Those that were afraid of the water flew.

Those that did not know how to swim or fly
floated back home,
they looked at the stars so long
that they memorized them,
the lights left marks on their bodies.

This is how the diaspora
knew
where to run.
The ones that became
ancestors
passed on the knowl-
edge to those
who could not go back
home at first.

Eventually,
they all came together again,
rejoiced and danced counterclockwise in circles

until the ancestral spirits rejoined them too,
until the skies heard their songs,

songs that were no longer about getting back to freedom

but about what to do
now that they had finally returned.

And they say that

after, they knew that sustaining themselves
meant honoring the Divinity
that had always been within them.

Now ain't that
somethin'.
Ain't it.

"Always and Forever," Love Alex

CHARLES RICE-GONZÁLEZ

T HE FIRST time I heard "Always and Forever" by Heatwave, I was in Alex's room and we were about to kiss. He had written down all the words to the song, put them in a sealed envelope that said "Private Open Later," and included it inside the birthday card he'd given me along with a bottle of Paco Rabanne cologne. I had turned fourteen years old. As I opened the private envelope, he told me it was a poem he'd written, and then confessed that it was a song and he wanted me to hear it.

It was 1978 and Michael Jackson was still Black like me. He also had a 'fro like me, and I loved my 'fro. I picked it out and patted it down to even it. I wanted to look good for Alex. I spritzed on a little of the cologne and in the privacy of my bathroom I read the lyrics to the song. The words floated off the page and made me dizzy. "Each moment with you is just like a dream to me that somehow came true."

Alex had been coming around our apartment a lot. I thought it was because of my cousin Carmela, who was sixteen, like him, and gorgeous, well, like him, too. They'd make a cute couple. Me and him? Well, in my mind we'd be perfect, but I knew I was in the minority.

He'd stare at me when no one was looking, almost as if he were in a trance. His dark green eyes made my heart play a different beat. No one had ever looked at me that way. After he'd go home from hanging out at our apartment listening to Fania and disco records, Carmela would tell me that she was into him and that he stared at her. I just nodded, although I wanted to blurt, "He stares at me, too," but I couldn't, and what if he wasn't? Maybe I wanted so badly for Alex to see me that I imagined that he did.

Alex and I had grown up in the same building in the Soundview Projects in the Bronx. He and his family, eight brothers and sisters, lived in an apartment across the hall. When we were little kids, his father would drive a bunch of us out to Orchard Beach, or we'd all go play in the big park down by the river. Alex loved salsa music and his favorite singer was Héctor

Lavoe. Alex sang his ballads like "Tus ojos," "Emborráchame de amor," and "De ti depende." I loved to sit and watch him sing.

"I was gonna write down a Héctor song," he told me, "but you are not into Spanish music, plus this Heatwave song, 'Always and Forever,' really speaks about how I feel about you." We entered the room he shared with his two brothers. The door didn't have a lock. His mother allowed us to be in the room with the door closed because we were both boys. My cousin Carmela couldn't be in this room even if Alex had wanted her to come (which he didn't).

He and I had been passing notes to one another for about two weeks. His first note read: "I like to look at you. I like to hang with you. How do you feel?" He'd spray his notes with his cologne, and before I read each one I'd inhale the notebook paper upon which they were carefully written. I kept them hidden inside my pillowcase, through which I could smell them when I slept. When I received that first note, my heart made itself known. His three simple lines were answered by a three-page letter that I had written, edited, and rewritten. I recall ripping up the drafts and flushing them down the toilet so no one would find them.

A few days later as he passed me in the hall, he slipped me another note. "I want you to be mine. I don't want your cousin Carmela, she is nothing to me. It's you that I need, baby. But we gotta keep it quiet. Nobody can know or it's over." Alex was a soap opera freak, and his favorite was *All My Children*. So his notes and actions always had a touch of melodrama.

I was so happy that I wanted to let the world know, but his note was clear: *Nobody can know or it's over.*

When we entered his room, it was no surprise that he had lit a candle, a religious kind with an image of San Lázaro on the front from his mother's altar. He had the needle to the record ready to land on the spot where the song was to begin. I sat on his bed. He closed the door. He turned off the light. The room glowed a cool indigo from the twilight sky. The flickering candlelight made our shadows dance. A faint whiff of garlic filled the air from the pollo guisao his mother had cooked that evening. The needle landed on the record and Heatwave's song oozed into the room. Alex extended his hand and led me to the door. "Lean against it in case somebody tries to come in." He extended his arms and pressed against the door facing me, each hand on either side of my head. With his face inches from mine, he smiled. He smelled like his letters. He craned his neck, tilted his head forward, and pressed his lips to mine. He bent his elbows, bringing his body closer, and pressed his crotch to mine, making slow circles in tune with the song's swirling rhythms.

We would have kissed for the entire extended twelve-inch version of the song had it not been for the push on the door. "Yo, what the fuck?" came from the other side of it. Alex quickly flicked on the light. I sat on the bed with my arms covering my crotch. Alex opened the door. Alex's older brother came in and grabbed a football that was under his bed. "What you two doing?"

"What does it look like?" Alex lifted the needle and started the song over.

"Y'all two need some girls up in here if y'all gonna be playing romantic shit like that." Then he looked at me and left. Alex let the record play as we sat side by side, holding the lyrics he had written and singing along with Heatwave. His voice was sweet and earnest.

After that night, stolen kisses followed—on stairwells, in my room, riding the elevator, inside the cement barrel at the big park—and the notes continued and were signed, *Always and Forever, Love Alex.*

Everyone knew us as best friends. "Those two are inseparable."

My cousin continued her attempts at wooing him. She asked him to take her roller-skating, to take her to the movies, to take her out to Central Park, but he refused. I always felt closer to him each time he rejected her.

One night, while we were in my living room listening to records and stealing glances, my cousin suggested that we listen to salsa. She was up to something.

"Alex, let's dance." One thing Carmela could do better than anyone I knew was dance salsa. Alex jumped up and they danced to one song and then another; by the fifth song I was in a quiet rage. I marched to my room, turned off the light, dived into my twin bed, and buried my head under the pillow. I could still smell his letters, and the scent intensified my pain. After they'd danced to what felt like two whole LPs of salsa music, they came looking for me.

"Charlie, you asleep?" Carmela sounded concerned.

"No." I held the pillow to my head.

"You OK?" Alex asked.

I peeked and saw their silhouettes in my doorway. "I have a stomachache."

She asked, "You want some Pepto?"

"OK."

"Can I talk to him in private, Carmela?"

"Sure."

I felt my bed sag as Alex sat next to me in the darkness. He placed a hand on my back. "It's you that I need." I tried to muffle my tears. He said, "Do you know that song? 'It's You That I Need' by Enchantment? The whole song is sad, but I love the chorus. It just repeats, 'It's you that I need.'"

I sobbed into my pillow, then he rested his head on my back. I continued to sob even though I was so happy to feel the weight of his head. His letters smelled good to me again, but I sobbed because this little moment of joy, cloaked in the darkness, would end when Carmela showed up with the Pepto.

But it didn't.

Alex sat up but continued to rub my back.

"Here's the Pepto."

Alex took it from my cousin. "Let me give it to him."

I didn't need it any longer, and besides, the pain wasn't in my stomach, but I swallowed the thick, chalky, minty liquid.

He handed the bottle and the spoon back to my cousin. "Let me sit with him a little while."

She left us. He got up and closed the door, because he could. We were both boys.

A thin line of light from the hall framed the door, and the soft streetlight allowed me to see him moving back toward the bed. My cousin had resumed playing salsa but it was low and distant. Was she trying to lure Alex back out?

He took my hand. "Get up, Charlie."

I stood in front of him. My eyes adjusted to the darkness and I could see his smile. He traced the contours of my face with his thumb. "You are so beautiful, negrito."

"Michael Jackson is cuter."

"Michael Jackson is nothing. I got you here with me." He embraced me. Then he started to slowly rock and sway. We danced as he hummed "Always and Forever." My face felt the vibration in his throat.

I moved with him, we found our rhythm easily. Even though the music drifting from the living room pulsed with percussion, soared with strings, and howled with horns, Alex and I undulated in each other's arms. "Alex?"

"Yes, papito?"

"Can we dance in the living room?"

He stopped. Pulled away a little. Looked at me, then resumed our slow dance. "If that's what you want, Charlie. Let's go dance."

"Really?"

He shrugged. "We got to sometime."

I hooked my arms around his shoulders. It felt so calm and peaceful to be swaying with him. But it wouldn't be so if we danced like this in the living room. "Can we wait just a little longer, Alex?"

"We can wait as long as we can."

I held him tighter and his humming became singing.

How to Draw a Memoir

BREENA NUÑEZ

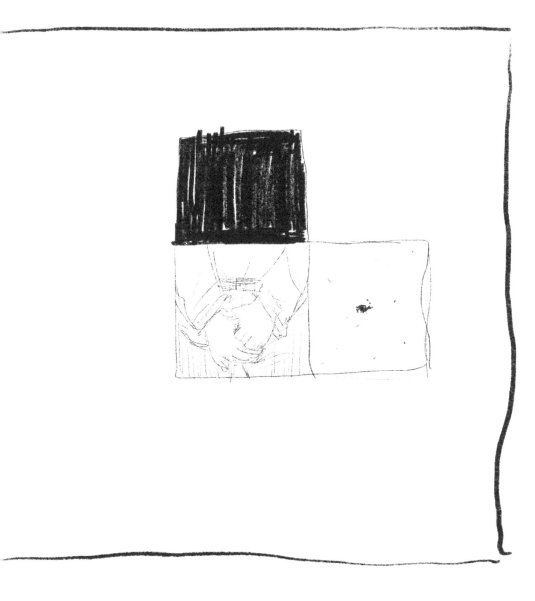

I REGRESS TO A TIME I LOATHED
SPEAKING, BECAUSE I KNEW WORDS THAT
CLUMSILY SPILLED OUT OF MY MOUTH.
I COULDN'T PAINT THE VISIONS TRAPPED
        IN   MY   HEAD. WORDS COULDN'T
CAPTURE HOW MAD I WAS AT WHITENESS.
THE PRESCRIPTION TO ONLY SPEAK ENGLISH FORCED ME TO
ABANDON A PLAYFUL LANGUAGE MY CHILDHOOD SELF CREATED.
IT COMPLIMENTED MY MINDs VISIONS; I FORGOT
HOW TO PAINT MY MUSIC IN COLOR.

IT WAS A FULL HOUSE AND I SHEEPISHLY GLIDED TO A SMALL TABLE. A NARROW BEAM OF LIGHT WAS BRIGHT ENOUGH FOR ME TO SET UP MY WORKSHOP.

A TIP ABOUT WRITING MEMOIR:
WRITE ABOUT SOMETHING THAT
MAKES YOU THE MOST UNCOMFORTABLE.

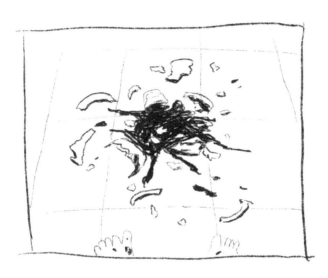

THEN A DAY OF GRIEVING IS
DEDICATED TO ALL PARTS OF THE SELF
THAT WASN'T "STRONG" ENOUGH TO
     CONTAIN THE DOWNPOUR.

Escaped Parrots Are Doing Lovely

JESSICA LANAY

A NEWSPAPER ARTICLE reports: *the escaped parrots are doing lovely* and thriving despite adapting to new climates. A parrot perches in a London plane tree, ruffling itself up around the neck as if wearing a lurid green winter coat. It seems natural: what does not adapt to what it cannot change is made to abide eventually. I am finding myself more resistant every day that I awake; more resentful of fending for myself through submission. This, too, is natural—I come from others who, like parrots, flourish on what to outsiders seem strange rituals. I am bored with the pattern of survival; tired of staving off hunger with laughter. Escapees are never seen as anything other than the opposition to their captivity. Those that have never had to escape anything will never overcome their fearful wonder. What would I do with ease and acceptance anyways?

CARE

Proximity, Intimacy, Togetherness

The masters
They woke up in the same house and they did not know her
They woke up and ate her food but they didn't know the taste of her
dreams
They woke up and told her child to be quiet but they didn't know the
sound of her anger
They woke up and told her to be awake as if they didn't know she
needed sleep

The mother
She woke up under the same sheets but didn't know her child tied the
fabric around her waist into illicit dresses.
She woke up in the same house but they didn't know the smells of the
house she longed to have as her own
She woke up in the same house but they didn't know her waking up
was her rebellion

The lover
He woke up in the same bed but he didn't know the texture of her heart
He woke up in the same bed but she wouldn't wake up again
He woke up in the same bed but he didn't know the actions to I love
myself and I love you

The child
She woke up in the same house but they didn't know the child was a
girl
She woke up in the same house but they pretended she was not there
She woke up in the same house and they didn't know her imagination
was her playground
She woke up in the same house but she didn't know she would come
from the future to hold her own hand

They all knew the closeness of distance

In my attempt to get closer, I asked
Mama, what did you do when your eyes were heavier than the world
outside of your body?
You wake up, my child
You wake up!

Love Thy Neighbor

SR. ÁLIDA

1 PETER 4:8

"Above all, love each other deeply, because love covers over a multitude of sins."

THE FIRST time I ate pussy, I was ten, maybe eleven. Esmeralda, la gordita del 3B.

Her family moved into our building in Villa Faro early summer '98 on the floor right above ours. Life was simple. I worried about simple things: picking up before Mami got home, not missing *La Mentira*, wondering when my titties would start poking out or why my pubic hair was growing in patches. Then she pulled up. Andaban en un camioncito azul, a single-cabin '87 Toyota pickup. Como el de los plataneros, but filled with their lives instead. She struggled off the truck juggling an oversized backpack stuffed full, a volleyball, a thick bible-looking book, and a white cat holding on for dear life to her hip.

Santo Domingo's skies were stripped of clouds. Ella parecía de porcelana: tall, thick, paled to paper. The sun bounced off her cheeks tinting them pink and she squinted away, the light unwelcome. Mamá Yaya and I played bríca on the front lot, hiding from the sun under a flamboyán. Ni saludaron. They moved quickly, quietly, not interrupting the afternoon, and they lived in the same way, careful not to move the trappings before them. From our post we watched them unload what little they brought: a stand-alone fan, two mattresses, a small round table, two chairs, a small television, and a few taped-up boxes. Her family was small. Three—well, four, if you counted Dionisio, their cat, mi pana from the jump, blinking a curious glare in my direction before the gate closed behind them.

"Pero ven acá, Camila, you playing or not?" Mamá Yaya's voice shook me from across the table.

"I'm about to, Mamá," I said, "don't rush me," but I kept daydreaming.

"Tú ve, that's why I can't play with you. Tira cualquier vaina ahí," she said before taking a long pull from her Marlboro Red, closing her eyes a moment then blowing the smoke at me. I breathed it in and chose my play.

Esmeralda and her folks made a few trips to unload the truck. She twirled across the parking lot right past us, and I followed the sound of her flip-flops echoing through the gate, down the hall, up the stairs, past my floor, to the last door on the right. Mamá Yaya took the game. I shuffled the deck.

The summer moved unbothered. I kept count of her every move at a distance, learning her routines and chasing the echo of her body breaking through the walls that divided us. From my bedroom window I could hear the novelas on her TV, her broken laughter, the volleyball bouncing from her bedroom wall, her stomping feet chasing after Dionisio. I'd imagine knocking on her door and joining her and Dionisio on their laps around the living room, but I never mustered the courage. Instead, I started plotting ways of casually bumping into her; camping out in the parking lot in case she ever came out, following her to el colmado when she did, and making sure I could pull off at least half a smile whenever we made eye contact. I was curious, hungry, swimming in a newness so present and so hurried, I struggled to find balance. When you're eleven, love lacks frames of understanding or concrete definitions. I was falling, though, right before her.

Eran testigos: Kingdom Hall on Sundays, Wednesday bible studies, Friday group prayers; no birthdays, no Christmas, no music. At most, Esmeralda sang hymns in the bathroom, and I listened embelesada, wanting things I'd yet to recognize. Mi familia wasn't particularly holy, Catholic by default. Mami tucked me in every night with a Padre Nuestro and two Ave Marías, but we only went to church if the Holy Ghost called us by name: weddings, baptisms, First Communions, and a funeral here and there. Enough to keep a safe distance from the gates of hell, but not quite enough to avoid its parting flames. Faith escaped me. I chased it all summer bouncing from hallway to hallway after Esmeralda. If I had to believe in anything, her big ole brown eyes round like pebbles and the thick-ass eyebrows above them sent me to pray. I waited, filled with the hope only first times can give.

By September, Mami and Marcela, Esmeralda's mom, had become friends: cafecitos por la tarde, mercado runs, a favor here, another there.

"Vecina, ¿me cuida la niña por una horita?" Marcela asked Mami to keep an eye on Esmeralda every Wednesday during bible study.

"Cami, take some habichuelas to Marcela for a little taste." Mami would send me over every time she made something she was proud of.

"¡Vecina, la ropa—va a llover!" they'd yerp out a weather warning through the service window.

They bonded over the loneliness of motherhood. Mami was still bitter about Papi's bitch-ass exit and Marcela was weighed down by a husband who was there but had stopped seeing her. They found solace in each other. They'd trade chismes about other neighbors and had long conversations about paradise and the afterlife. Mami stared blankly, gliding between Marcela's words always flooded with such enamoring conviction. Yet Mami's faith bordered the well. She leaned over the edge sometimes, but never leapt in.

"Camila, you're going with Marcela to Kingdom Hall on Wednesday," she'd tell me every so often after chatting with Marcela, trying to get me on the path to sanctification. Their talks always shook Mami's faith. She never visited Kingdom Hall or gave up on the Pope, but she always came back weary of salvation and took measurements—however minimal—to keep us saved.

School started de un día pa' otro. Esmeralda went to La Gregorio Luperón, a public school in our neighborhood. I knew because some days we'd drive by her on our way to my school, swaying in her khaki skirt and tucked-in button-up. She caught a motoconcho on the corner of La San Vicente with the rest of the neighborhood kids. Every time we'd drive by, Mami would warn me I'd be joining them soon, if Papi didn't come out his pocket with child support. Mami was still paying for El Víctor Manuel on the other side of the city. She was struggling, though. The school secretary would hand me the notices to take home at least once a week.

I started bumping into Esmeralda in the emergency staircase after school, but she never said anything beyond a hello and a smile. Neither did I. One afternoon I was feeling brave and brought her un frío frío de limón.

"You like frío frío?" I asked her.

"Claro." She looked back on her way up the stairs. "¿Ese es pa' mí?"

"If you want it," I responded.

"Call me Nani," she told me, "that's what my friends call me."

"So we're friends in real life?" I asked jokingly.

"Maybe." She giggled in a way that made my throat tickle.

"I'm Camila, Cami for short," I mumbled nervously, never making eye contact.

"Camila José," she said confidently.

"Waitaminute—how you know?" I was surprised.

"Doña Yaya yells it out the window enough for the whole residencial to know." She wasn't lying.

"You can sing." The words streamed out of my chest after weeks of faithful audience.

"You heard me?" she asked, raising her left eyebrow firmly my way.

I didn't want her to know that I'd been listening, lying on my back staring at the ceiling imagining her octave breaking through me. I pulled back embarrassed, leaning my shoulder against the hallway wall. She smiled and leaned in. She knew I'd been listening then, but what's worse: I knew she knew.

We met on the emergency staircase every afternoon, talked about all and nothing, played with Dionisio, she'd warn me about seventh grade, I'd complain about fifth. She liked bows on her hair and wore them all the time, shifting between a scruffy side ponytail and two wavy pigtails on each side of her ears. I hated brushing my hair. My kinks fought against any disruption to their free form. I rarely fought back.

Nani liked playing with my earlobe. She'd sit beside me, move my hair out of the way, and rub on my ear as she talked about her day. Her fingers whispered softly, dozing me out. No one, aside from Mamá Yaya, ever touched me so gently. Everything grew in such a way, calmly, uninterrupted, lust unceasingly bursting inside me, against my will or ability to recognize it: *Prepubescent Wet Dreams: A True Story.*

Le enseñé a jugar bríca y yax. She learned fast and soon started beating me every time. She tried, unsuccessfully, to get me jumping rope, but my lungs weren't cut out for it. I was clumsy, chubby, and too worried about breaking a sweat in front of her. I didn't learn, but we had fun trying. Our days turned to months like run-on sentences, no punctuation, playdates, weekends in el campo with Mamá Yaya, infinite late-night chatters breaking through the crickets' harmony. I kept falling.

One day after school I saw her cutting through the parking lot hand in hand with Miguelito, el negrito del 5C. I watched from the balcony as they giggled and fiddled their way into the building, losing them at the entrance where my eyes could no longer reach. That afternoon she told me, hyped as fuck, that Miguelito asked her out, but she was "thinking about it, you know, you can't make it too easy on 'em." Pero, ¿y cuándo fue eso? Where was I? I panicked.

I was angry, but the sadness was more. If I had a chance, it ended with Miguelito. More words stumbled eagerly between her teeth. I heard nothing. The "us" I had sheltered myself behind undid itself before me. She, on the other hand, was happy, painfully so.

"Should I tell Mami? ¿Tú crees que se quille?" she asked excitedly.

I shrugged. She kept talking. I faded away.

It took me a minute, but I pretended shit was cool. I told her I was sick and skipped the staircase for a couple days. At the time, I wasn't too sure where the ache came from or if the feeling of loss had any real meaning.

Days later we met again and sat beside each other on the steps. Dionisio had gotten shots and laid his body heavily on Nani's side. She smelled like oatmeal. I, to be honest, was on the much mustier side. El sol aún estaba picando, bared of clouds to break its path. Our thighs glued together in sweaty patches of heat, we didn't move, though, laughing and frolicking with one another. My neck melted into a stream down my chest where my shirt started to stick. She played with my bead bracelet, I wrote on her knee cap, namelessly building up.

Her eyes smiled at me like a dare, and my heartbeat rose to the top of my throat. And so we kissed. Well, I kissed her. She wanted me to, I think. I took the chance in a quiet moment. She stopped her eyes on mine with a grinning invitation, and I just, well, I kissed her. And she kissed me back for a few seconds; shut-eye, wet, unsorted, naïve, a question more than a kiss, a finding. I lived in her softness those few seconds, a home better than I'd imagined, a pathway. She breathed in between my breaths, tickling my lips with her mustache. Home it was, pero qué poco duró. She pulled away, and I watched her speed into the hallway. I sat at the top of the stairs without moving, wishing she'd look back at me. She didn't.

I waited faithfully, but Nani stopped coming out. I wanted to apologize, to take it all back, hold off on my move and maybe not move at all. We'd done something wrong. I'd done something wrong. I struggled to name what.

1 CORINTHIANS 6:9-10

"Or do you not know that wrongdoers will not inherit the kingdom of God? Do not be deceived: Neither the sexually immoral nor idolaters nor adulterers nor men who have sex with men nor thieves nor the greedy nor drunkards nor slanderers nor swindlers will inherit the kingdom of God."

And what if I kissed a girl?

Mami used to say I was different. Hollow, ain't it? I wonder what she meant. As I grew into myself, I started unthreading. Slowly, but steadily, coming undone. I told no one about Esmeralda. I knew not to. In Villa Faro,

lesbianism was an invisible monster, hidden carefully away from the inno-
cent eye. Our novelas weren't about Marías holding hands. Our love stories
never had Cleo and Úrsula kissing against the hood of a car. So what, then,
set off this unquenchable fire? Villa Faro was all I'd known.

In Mami's house, gayness always followed an explanation: "Your tío Julio
was like that, good peoples, but he died of AIDS," or, "Hardworking, pero
maricón, you know? ¡Que Dios lo tenga en su gloria!" I had no explanation.
Nothing yet to shape these feelings. No clear articulation of who or what I
was just a moment ago between Nani's lips.

I sought mirrors outside myself and bumped into a collective erasure,
doubtful I even existed. Loneliness is a strong bitterness when you can't
find yourself outside yourself. Loneliness is a deep river when you're eleven;
your toes wiggle at the surface not finding the bottom.

Un domingo, after weeks of silence, Nani came down to get me.

"¿Vamo' pa' mi casa?" she invited me.

I can't remember if I answered, but I followed her down the hall, up
the stairs, and into their apartment. We were alone. She skipped Kingdom
Hall that morning. I overheard Marcela ask Mami to keep an eye on Nani.
Something about "a lice breakout at bible camp" and "Nani staying home
to be on the safe side."

"Ta to, what we about to do?" I stood at her door unmoving, a bit nervous and even more confused.

"¡Camina, ven!" She pulled me through the living room, past the bathroom, and into her bedroom. *Yo Amo a Paquita Gallego* was on. "Vamo' a
ver la novela," she told me.

Her room was bright, airy. The sun crept through her curtains, painting
the walls. La magia de siempre, except the newness of our first kiss drowning every thought, every move, taking up space, closing us in. Dionisio
lay on the bed. We sat facing each other on the floor, our palms pressed
together as if in prayer. Y ahí hicimos misa.

I can't be sure where we began. Her leg extended over mine, she smiled, I
smiled, I leaned in for a tap, she laid one on me. Her hands rushed unsettled
all around my body, under my shirt, on my back, on my neck, behind my
head, inside my shorts. I worried—about the hair patches, my flat chest, the
heat rushing down my thighs (sweat, lust, both), about Mami downstairs,
about Miguelito el del 5C, about Peter and Corinthians. I worried. I prayed.
She kissed me.

Her fingers pressed against my crotch, motioning in circles left and right.
My clit swelled against them through the panties and shorts, growing into the

novelty of the moment. My knees locked and my breath thickened—angsty, confused, not understanding my body or my desires. I followed her lead, shaking in her hands y baboseándole la cara. Time echoed slowly around us. Soon we were naked from the bottom down. Her toto wasn't like mine. Su toto no tenía frente, no mountain to climb. I didn't have to search for her parts, they rose to the surface. Nani's pubic hair was long and fine, perfectly covering her lips. She grabbed my hand and pressed it against her clit, mimicking what she'd done on mine a moment before. Her wetness leaked between my fingers, gluing them together while also helping them glide.

"¿Qué hago?" I asked, my nervous stare meeting her before my words.

"Kiss it," she said through a soft smirk.

I was scared. Once, in Mami's room, I played a video she'd forgotten on the VHS. It was less than three minutes before I got caught, but it was three minutes too long. A lady lay on the couch wide-legged, and a man kneeled in front of her. He fingered her toto hardcore and French-kissed it between pumps. Felicia, la trabajadora, walked in on me and told Mami. I was grounded for the rest of the summer. I hated the stupid video until this moment. ¿Qué sabía yo que los totos eran para mamarse? Nani lay in front of me wide-legged too, her pubic hair visibly damped, her breaths rushed twice as fast as mine, waiting for me to do something, anything. And so, I did. I leeched my lips on her clit and kissed it, slobbering on my chest and gripping onto her thighs. The floor helped cool our bodies. La novela drowned her gasps for air.

I was stuck on Nani when Marcela opened the door. She found us on the floor naked, Nani spilling from the edges of my mouth, her panties wrapped around her ankle, mine somewhere on the floor. She pulled Nani by the elbow, y a mí ni me miró. I picked up what I could and ran my ass home. Dignity escaped me. Fermín, her dad, stood at the door waiting for me to get out. I did, head down, y sin mucho ruido.

2 PETER 3:17

"You therefore, beloved, knowing this beforehand, be on your guard so that you are not carried away by the error of unprincipled men and fall from your own steadfastness."

I rushed into the shower unnoticed. Mami was asleep on the couch. For the next hour, I scrubbed Nani off my body: every look, every smile, every touch, every sweat patch, su olorcito a avena, all the desires that rested on my belly. I prayed all night; if only I hadn't looked at her, if only she hadn't looked back. I prayed all night that Marcela wouldn't tell Mami and that she wouldn't whip Nani too hard. I prayed all night; as if praying hard enough would turn back time, bring me to a beginning where Nani wasn't. I prayed all night and found no prayer to rid my body of this sin, to help reconcile the feelings of joy and shame that danced inside me.

Nani went ghost for the next couple of weeks. There were no hymns flying out of her bathroom window, no novelas sounding off her television, and no stomping feet on her floors. I saw her a few times at the motoconcho stop with Miguelito and them, but she never came back to the emergency staircase again.

They moved out the following summer, loading their little pickup as quietly as they came. I watched them from the balcony. Cogieron to'a La San Vicente. She sat between Marcela and Fermín, squashed inside the one cabin. I watched until they disappeared, herded through the evening's traffic. Parecían hormiguitas mientras se me escapaban.

Collaborative Poems

JANICE HEATHER HECTOR (ST. LUCIA) AND
FELENE M. CAYETANO (BELIZE)

I N MAY 2020, two friends of friends were challenged to pretend to be in an ideal relationship with each other for one week. These are two poems that emerged from the pretend union, since both writers are seasoned poets. Neither had previously met the other in person or online, although they had been told about each other over time, as happens in Caribbean artistic and LBT circles.

WAKE UP
If this is a dream
only wake me up
if you'll be in bed beside me.
Otherwise let's stay here
skin to skin
limb to limb
wrapped in afterglow.
If this is a dream
nobody haffi know
why I choose to stay here.
The smile will tell them
I'm in bliss.

Mmmmmmmmm!

I hope I'm not moaning
with each longing lingering kiss.

Wake up, Queen!
It's no longer a dream.
My Love
I am right beside you
with desires to feel you skin to skin
to be entangled between these sheets
to embrace you limb to limb.
I am that dream
your soul has been craving.
Let me arouse your desires
Right now, right here
and yes, my smile will tell them
that in you
I've found my bliss.
So who cares if I am moaning
your touch humbles me like this.
What honey is there sweeter than
your longing
lingering
kiss?

MANY LOVES
When I said I had eyes only for you
you never did believe me.
Yes I flirted with this other woman
but our conversations
didn't become reality.
I watched her lips beg my name
I admit my heart did flutter
but it is you who breathes
my heart to beat
it is to your love
I have surrendered.
How many sorries must I admit

to heal your wounded soul?
For only your love can heal my brokenness
I hate that our bed feels cold.
. . .
You know I've been hurt before
felt like I had a true one
but she only had my back
when she was hitting it
from the back.
I don't mind your flirtation
in fact she's gorgeous
threesome temptation.
It's too early for that though
we have to water what we have
give us time to grow.
My soul's not wounded
because I have a crush too.
The thing is
she lives close to you.
They say two is company
three is a crowd
four sounds like an orgy
unless there's jealousy.
Queen, can we please agree
to delay our polyamory?

Free

RAQUELLE MAYORAL

I dream of your clit inside my mouth. Hands
filled with hope and molasses and honor.

We sit on a curb discussing life after graduation,
whose family expects
marriage and grandbabies
whose family will be extinct.

Your dreams are like mine.
Embracing:
          kindness   love   truth.

Your body fades into mist. I wake
and smell your cum on my fingers.
Only street light shines my lonely.

My dreams are like:
          yours? she can never be.

The Uncertainty of Feelings for Girls

RAQUELLE MAYORAL

keep it to myself. fold it up—
like the origami crane Judah gave
me on the last day of third grade.
put it in the chest pocket
of my favorite blue jean shirt. forget,
and let Momma wash it, sudsy warm.

Hurricane Marlene

LORRAINE AVILA

"¡Mi'ja! ¡Marlene!" Mama Marta screams from inside the house as I turn off the motorcycle. Tío Marte is standing over la vieja and Marlon is sitting on a rocking chair looking pissed. *Fuck.* It's always some type of telenovela drama going on in this family. Can't even take my girl to a nice lunch without coming back to a burning house. I planned it and everything, paid Charo, a trusted neighbor we often bring clothes to whenever we return to the Island, to care for la vieja for a couple hours. Marlene sweeps her right leg off the back seat and runs up the driveway. I follow her, opening up my water bottle and taking a few gulps.

Mama Marta reaches for Marlene, and Marlene crouches besides her. "He was trying to force me." The vieja's bony finger points at Marlon.

"Force her to do what?!" Marlene looks up at Marlon.

"Ya, Marlene, let it go," Tío Marte, Marlene's godfather, says.

"You were trying to get her to do what?" Marlene yells again. She takes her eyes off of Marlon and looks at Charo.

"Ay Marlene," Charo whines. "I had to go to the bathroom. Yo salí volando because I heard la vieja screaming. When I came out, he was holding her hand, there was a pen, he was trying to get her to sign something."

Marlene stands up, snatches the water bottle out of my hand, positions her stance like a quarterback, and flings it. The stainless steel water bottle hits her target's face and the water spills all over Marlon. As the tíos gasp, sucking in all the air around them in surprise, they tell on themselves—they haven't internalized that the women in the Vargas family don't sleep. They ain't sheep. And they definitely ain't like they are in my familia: all mouth and no hands.

"¡Mira, coño, maldita loca!" Marlon growls. He immediately crowns the coffee mug in his right hand with his grip. I flinch, knowing for a fact that his only goal is to shatter it on my girl's face. I want to react, but I am glued to the ground beneath me. Tío Marte holds his brother's arm and urges him to relax. "The police chief is all over this," Marlon whispers as he pulls the wet cotton off of his chest.

"Go ahead, call him, you fucking thief, maldito abusador," Marlene snarls. She moves a chair closer to her grandmother and sits, crossing her legs and placing her hand over the vieja's bony fingers as they share the armrest. From where I stand, the resemblance is obvious—Marlene is Mama Marta born again with three times the fire Marta is said to have had in her youth. If my own grandmother had been open about all she endured in Nicaragua, would I be able to react in moments like this? The first time Marlene fought with a family member in front of me I froze, like I used to freeze when Papi used to beat my mother like it was nothing. Instead of doing something, like crying, I'd stay in place, pretend nothing was happening. Sometimes, after I could move, I would head to the kitchen. That night when we were alone, after Marlene fought with her family in front of me for the first time, I asked her if she needed anything out of me in those moments. She looked at me and laughed a little before saying, "I was raised to fight. You were raised to hold the ground below our feet. All I need of you is for you to keep doing that for me."

There are big trails of sweat falling down Marlene's forehead. "We can finally put you in prison for falsifying your dead father's name on the deeds to the land," she begins. "You know the real reason you're not rotting in there yet is because of your sisters, cause I have no problem seeing you in there."

"Don't say that, Marlene," Tío Marte responds. Tío Marte is the only man with some kindness in his heart in this family. The only one who hasn't stolen land from his own kin since the women all migrated to the States.

Marlon laughs hysterically, leans back in his plastic chair, opens his thick legs wider. "That land is rightfully mine. Who works it? You talk—"

"The Haitians, the campesinos in Arroyo Torro. Please don't try me." Last time we came to the Dominican Republic, Mama Marta had us go check in on the land. She said she was having dreams of roosters falling onto it from the sky and fighting until only one was left. When we arrived, the farmer in charge complained about not being able to pay those tending the land, because Marlon wasn't keeping his word on when he'd pay.

Marlene fixes the waistband of her pants. She glances at me and raises an eyebrow, sorry but not embarrassed that I'm a witness to this. I smirk. I am amused and frankly turned on by the armor she takes off only when it's time for me to cradle her in the dark.

The Jeep Wrangler pulls into the driveway and the hermanas step out. For a hot minute, the universe twirls around them. Being in this family is really like being in a telenovela, and goddamn, I stay entertained. The dark dogs loose in the backyard run to the driveway. Marandrissa steps out of the front seat in flip-flops and her heels dangling off her fingers. Marpilar, Marlene's mother, takes off her dark Chanel sunglasses as she walks toward the house. Her trousers are high on her waist and her steps, in six-inch heels, are hardly calculated. After Marandrea turns off the car, she drops the gun she keeps in the safety compartment in her Coach bag and slams the door to the Jeep. My own tías and mother are also in their fifties and sixties, but they haven't reclaimed aging like the Vargas women have.

"Mi'ja, who are those women?" Mama Marta whispers loudly to Marlene.

"Your daughters, Marpilar, Marandrea, and Marandrissa," Marlene says. She repeats their names every day, countless times. Mama Marta remembers only her third grandchild and her late husband when the dementia is at its heaviest. "On that other side, you have your sons. Marte and Marlon; Marandres must be elsewhere selling some other solar."

Mama Marta grunts at the men. "Men are no go—" La vieja coughs. Coughs. Coughs. I run into the kitchen, grab a tissue, and bring it back quickly. Marlene takes it and wipes her grandmother's mouth.

"Marlene, leave the vieja out of esa mierda," Marpilar says, leaning down to greet her brothers. Her tank top shows off the cuts on her arms gained from mopping for wealthy folks in New York and hitting the gym four times a week before work.

"And you?" Marpilar says, looking down at Marlon. "What hurricane hit you?" The yellow button-up shirt sticks to his shoulder and resembles melted bizcocho ice cream from Helados Bon. The fourth tía, Marilar, enters from her usual afternoon visit to el colmado, with a white foam cup in her hand. I dab eucalyptus oil on the back of my ears and suck in the scent.

"Hurricane Marlene," Marlene declares. "And that's nothing. I got waves and high wind coming in, que no se apure." Marilar laughs as she walks in, her bag hanging from her right shoulder. She gives her niece a high five and walks past her brothers without greeting them.

"Mala?" Mama Marta whispers to Marlene. It's a nickname her brothers had given Marilar after she threw a rock at Marlon's face when she was just three; the scar still shines like a jagged crystal on the bottom left corner of his cheek. "That's her," Marlene confirms.

"That's who you got it from—the fight. We all have a sprinkle of it, the women. I made sure mi Santa gave us that. But that one," la vieja says, rubbing the side of her chin with a shaking finger, "le dio agua de beber a estos hombres." Mama Marta looks around. "But coño, she was mean, but she got distracted easily, so she couldn't do it either."

"Do what, Mama?" Marlene asks.

"Focus enough to drown the poison out of them," la vieja whispers, unaware of the fact everyone can hear her. I laugh as I bring a plastic chair next to Marlene. "These men, they're not alright, Marlene." Mama Marta rubs her wrist and shoots a bullet into Marlon with her eyes. "I couldn't take them on by myself, but God," the vieja points to the sky, "knows I tried."

"I'll finish the job, Mama."

"You promise?"

"I promise. I will drive the greed out of them, or I'll drown them," Marlene whispers back. La vieja squeezes Marlene's hand, turns her shrinking, smiling face up to kiss her granddaughter. It is these moments, when Mama Marta's memory comes back, that Marlene uses as evidence to prove la vieja is still in her right mind.

"It's time for a bath, Mama," Marlene says, pretending to be disgusted by her grandmother's body odor. I finger the ring in my pocket. *Yes God, bring in the joy. Please don't let this man fuck up my engagement.*

Mama Marta laughs like a child. Then the cough comes again, a dry cough that threatens to break her breath.

I met Marlene on the Island. She was sitting alone with a book at an Instagram-worthy café in Jarabacoa I was visiting with my cousins. It was only my second time in the Dominican Republic, and only the third time in my life spending time with my father's family. After Mami finally left him when I was nine, he disappeared from both of our lives.

I couldn't keep my eyes off of Marlene when I saw her; maybe it was the way she came in with a fresh Caesar and a loud red lip, maybe it was the way the bronzed brown of her shoulder glowed. Maybe I knew then one day I'd want to marry her. My primo, Yayson, went over to kick it to her, and she told him straight up: "I don't like men. Y menos los hombres relambío." She was like that from the get-go, always a strong surge of winds. When he came back like someone who had narrowly avoided drowning, I laughed. On our way out, she stopped me and slipped her number into my back pocket.

That night we went for dinner, and then I drove her back to her Airbnb. When she invited me in, she told me her family was from Bonao, but she had taken four days to come to Jarabacoa and clear her head. Her family was driving her up the wall and she just needed a moment to catch herself. We watched episodes of the new season of *Dear White People*. She filled up the bathtub in her room with hot water and bubbles.

"I'm such a fake activist using heated water to fill up a tub in a Third World country, right?" she whispered. With the tips of her fingers she whirled the water into small cyclones.

I shook my head, leaned my face on the white porcelain edge of the tub, and looked up at her. "We all deserve nice things."

"Violet," Marpilar calls. I turn to see my mother-in-law. My hands are elbow deep in dishes. I told the lady who helps out to let me do them, it's how I self-care sometimes. It's how I learned to self-soothe after the violence, how I escaped the dullness of my mother's family for a long time after we moved in with my grandmother and my mother's siblings—instead of sitting and watching Telemundo for hours to avoid one another, I turned to the dishes. "You can't control Marlene?"

Marlene is a thing too sure of her existence to be tamed. It isn't like she walks around at full strength, but there's something about her family that escalates her—makes a level-four natural disaster from the jump.

"She wouldn't listen even if I tried, and anyway, she has a right to feel every way she does. I try to stay out of it, but what that man did to Mama Marta is not OK." Marlene is the way she is with her family because she loves them, she wants to destroy them so that they are pushed to change. But I can't tell Marpilar that shit.

"Are you feeling nervous?" Marpilar whispers, changing the subject. She came with me to pick out the engagement ring weeks before the trip. I wanted to invite Mami as well, but she isn't here for it. She truly did pray for the fact I love women to be a phase.

"A little. She's not in a good mood," I respond. I pray by tomorrow Marlene won't be this angry, so she feels like she wants everyone there when I drop to my knees.

"Yeah, well, you know my daughter," she laughs. "You better hold on because it's all high winds from here." She pops a bit of batata Marilar roasted into her mouth and laughs her way back out onto the balcony. I shake my head at this woman acting like she wasn't the one who raised Marlene to be a storm.

I am drying the dishes when Marlon comes by and takes a cup of boiling milk to drink with the batata. As he brings the spoon from the caldero to the top of the mug, I try to search for the softness Marlene said she once saw in him. Other than the scar, his face is clear, not a blemish or sunspot in sight like the other brothers, not a wrinkle, despite the fact he is one of the oldest.

"You clean," he says. Maybe a joke, maybe something to fill the air.

"You're dry," I note.

"Marlene es una loca. It makes sense she had to stop dating men," he says.

"That's funny. I find no sense in why you have to keep stealing from your own family to make sure your wife doesn't leave," I respond, surprising myself. He looks at me like I just killed his firstborn.

I wasn't always this quick. I learned to stay safe by keeping quiet, by pretending not to see, not to feel. But Marlene trained me to say the things I have to say when I have to say them even when I have to say them to her.

Marlon scoops the top layer off of the milk and pours it into his cup.

Here's what they don't tell you: taking back power always comes with a direct loss. Like joining the Illuminati—you've got to give up a powerful human relationship. Because connections—that's the shit that counts.

Marlene's childhood albums have Marlon all over them. Her small legs spread over his motorcycle, he held onto her with a smile so wide anyone would've thought she was his own. During the summers the sisters sent the kids back to the Island, Marlon hit his other nieces and nephews when they stepped out of line, but never Marlene. Never la niña. Nothing was ever her fault. Until she told on him. He took her with him to la gallera one time and when Marpilar asked him where the money she had sent him to pay the accumulated debt en el colmado had gone, Marlene said he had spent it betting on roosters and buying rum for the other betters. She was eight. He scolded her in private. "You can't be trusted," he said to her. For a long time, she believed it. Believed her voice was a tool that leads to ruin. She never forgot. Neither did he.

"Babe, you don't have to dry all this shit. They don't do that here," Marlene says. She's been putting the vieja down for the last hour.

"Self-soothing," I say.

"Sorry there are so many moving parts," she says. She apologizes knowing damn well I find my grounding easiest when there is chaos.

"I'm going to go pick up the cousins with Padrino. You coming?"

I take a deep breath, put down the rag. "I'm coming."

My blood pours out of SDQ in slides and socks. Walking dollar signs even when they don't try. We speak in the same Dominican lingo and accent and yet it doesn't mask the fact that the majority of our years are spent on soil that comes with another type of freedom, one it would take generations for the average person here to find. We had each paid for the American dream twenty times over with nothing to show for it yet. Pero that does not matter to those that stare at us. And how could it? We have access. Un flow diferente. Like they say in el barrio, eso se huele. You can smell the scent of privilege even when there's sweat.

My uncle throws me the keys to his pickup truck and a group of us jump in. The other two groups crowd into rented SUVs. As soon as we're all in, we get on the road. The bachata is loud and the windows are low until the scent of burning garbage forces me to put them up.

"¡Marlene, hay hambre!" one of my cousins yells from the backseat.

"Say less," I respond. All airlines be giving nowadays is a bag of chips on the plane. I direct the lineup of vehicles behind me into the driveway of a comedor on the carretera I've heard is decent.

"Mami, what can I serve you?" the woman behind the counter asks. She taps her short French nails on the counter.

"Give me," I turn to count the heads. There are eleven of us, including Marnelis and Marerick's kids. "Six Presidente Jumbos, cinco jugos de chinola, three orders of pica pollo con frito and three orders of pica pollo with fries."

The men bring together three square plastic tables, and Violet and I shuffle around relocating extra chairs. As soon as we're sitting, the conversation swells the place. The summer has been nothing but work in New York, the jobs taking priority despite the heat. There have been breakups, reconciliations, and the realities of parenthood have slapped a few of my cousins in the face the minute the grandparents went away.

"Well, fuck it, here's to a lit Patio summer," I say. Our Presidente-filled plastic cups come together in a celebratory cheers midair.

Marbely brings her dark curls into a high ponytail. She creates a fan out of the menu.

"How are the uncles?" she asks.

"How you think?" I begin. "Being thieves. Killing Mama. Just the other day I had to fight Tío Marlon cause I found him holding down Mama's hand to sign a deed to a land he was trying to sell behind everyone's back. When I confronted him he tried to act like I'm crazy!"

"What an asshole."

"Yeah, I hope some of ya can help out cause I'm tired of always being the one," I say, taking a swig of her beer. My cousins relate to Mama Marta's suffering in a way I can't always understand. Don't they feel it? Aren't they pushed to violence because of it?

"Have you seen Rodrigo and them?" Martin asks, sitting back in his chair. I nod. Tell them how Violet and I have gone to Papaya's with them a few times only to end up paying to get Rodrigo out of drunken fights. Twice.

"Shit is probably set up," Violet says, her hands in her pocket. Everyone nods, not doubting that Rodrigo would do all that to get a cut of a few dollars. "Wouldn't surprise me," Marelias says.

"How's what's-his-face, the dude we used to go watch in el play? Coño, I'm blanking. It's the mom brains," Marnelis says. Because she's been busy making kids for the last three years, we haven't really filled her in. She holds her newborn baby girl in the crook of her right arm and swoops her swollen breast into her mouth. It isn't the hormones. Most of us had all pretended to forget his existence. Junjun had not come through the family house in años. Even though we had all come up like nail and finger, he didn't have the balls to come through and face everyone. Unlike my cousin, who I had to tolerate, he wasn't blood. There was no space for him in The Forgiveness.

"Junjun?" Mariposa says. The congregation goes silent. Violet raises an eyebrow at me and then brings down her gaze. Her way to tell me to reflect before I respond. I've told her everything. She knows what it is. I don't have no feelings for the dude, but my cousin's betrayal still stings. I don't know why, but ever since I found out what she was capable of when I was younger, I just want to burn shit down, and Violet—she helps me direct my energy in a way I need.

"Junjun!" Marnelis exclaims. The baby's eyes flutter as sleep comes for her.

Mariposa leans her torso onto the table. She takes a swig from her cup. Our eyes connect only when her pinky finger extends. She is the eldest, pushing forty and the epitome of silent confidence. Her twenty-four-inch bundles fall in waves down her soft back fat. Tall and wide. Our parents fat-shamed her into her late twenties and, after a failed bypass surgery, finally learned to accept her. Mariposa loves food and drinking. Despite her psychology degree, she would be the last to admit that most of her desires are connected to her trauma. I don't blame her. All her life she's had to cover it up. When Tía Marandrea went in for seven years, it was Mariposa who had to raise her younger sister Marbely and baby brother Martin. It was Mariposa who had to show up at her father's Otra's house to ask for money. She was the one that had to sit through court cases with the witnesses describing all the shit her parents were caught up in. It was her mother taking the hit to avoid her father being deported that got Mariposa to guilt-trip him into at the very least sleeping at their house so that child services wouldn't take her siblings away. Mariposa skipped the cocoon, went straight to adult bug. It wasn't easy. And it shows, it's always shown.

Tío Marlon likes to say that even as adults, we tend to follow her around; the chicken and her baby chicks, he nicknamed us. But there was a code she helped us build and maintain: loyalty for the family above all else. It's how we all lived.

Junjun was the first boy I consented to fucking me. In other words, Junjun was the first person I loved. I was twelve, so maybe it didn't mean anything then, but we fucked deep into my senior year in high school. And if I hadn't gotten so caught up in college, I would've kept my half-ass childhood promise of marrying him and bringing him over. I never told him I would, but I told myself. That meant something.

Every summer our mothers shipped us off to El Patio. And every summer, for three straight months, Junjun and I were a thing. He'd stroll up my family driveway in the heat of the afternoon smelling like sweat, his baseball cap always tinted by dirt. And then he'd come back after dinner cleaned up, smelling up the air around him in cheap cologne, and we played dominos, *musa-musa tátara musa*, talked shit, and drank beer until Papa told us it was time for bed. Watching Junjun take swings at the air around us with an invisible bat as he walked away always made me wet. It was Mariposa who helped me sneak out after everyone was asleep in the same ways she had sneaked out to fuck his brother. Mariposa used to lend me the flashlight to light the way as I went through the side of the house to the back of the mango tree. Mariposa was the one who would tell me where her condoms were when I ran out of my own. It was Mariposa who I came to with el chisme when I heard Junjun had a girlfriend en el callejón donde él vivía. When the girl, Lorena, marched down her barrio with a colín to try and cut me on my way to the colmado, it was Mariposa who threw a rock at the back of her head so we could take her down. Mariposa was the one who told me to enjoy him while I had him and forget the rest.

"But what about loyalty?" I asked once.

"Loyalty is reserved for blood. Los hombres no son de nadie." That was the lesson, or so I thought.

I didn't go back to the Island for a good six years. College had me busy, then grad school, and frankly I wanted to see other places. Plus, Mama and Papa had gotten their residency and they was coming two or three times a year. When the cousins would come on their own, they would bring back bits of information. Junjun inherited some money. Junjun got married to Lorena. Junjun had a baby girl. Junjun estaba eplotao because Lorena overfed him to keep him locked to his house. He hit me up on WhatsApp this one time confessing his love, and I told him straight up, "Eso es cosa del pasao. But you are always going to be someone I grew up with." After he called me desgraciada a few times and sent voice notes playing Luis Vargas lyrics, I stopped replying.

Papa's funeral was what got us all back to the Island together. I, having been the only one who hadn't visited, was surprised by the way the Island had shrunk.

Without Papa around, the jokes around the house were nonexistent. Grief hits my family right on the partying bone, so there wasn't much to be said when the whole gang of cousins appeared in Papaya's the night after the burial. I only recognized Junjun because he still had the same pelotero walk even though he was pushing weight and because he whispered, "Finally my mujer is here," into my ear. ¡Qué asco! Not only was he not attractive anymore, but he had a whole family and had the nerve to be trying to claim someone he hadn't seen in ages—wack.

"I can't believe I was into him," I whispered to my cousins on our way home. Mariposa laughed. "You were in love with him though," she said. I pretended to puke in my own mouth.

Every night, Junjun would come with us to the club. I danced with him a few times, but then he started gripping my ass. So I stopped dancing with him all together. "Comparona. You really think you hot shit?" he hissed into my ear the first time I denied him. Mariposa is a great salsa dancer, so I wasn't surprised when "La Rebelión" came on and he pulled her out onto the dance floor.

Three days later, I went to Picota, the neighborhood barber. After an hour's wait, I sat on his worn-out chair.

"A one and a half," I said. He nodded. All the men stared as my short curls hit the floor. A few of them extended their condolences. Stories of my grandfather, the only farmer known in El Cibao to cure cattle like nobody's business.

"They don't make men like el doctor no more," one of them said.

Wass, another childhood friend, entered the barbershop. He greeted everyone and then pretended to faint when he saw me.

"You are a grown-ass woman now!" He smiled. I nodded. He caught me up on his job delivering milk from my grandfather's finca to the rest of the town. Told me he had his eyes on a plot of land that belonged to his family decades ago.

"Ven acá, Marlene, wasn't Junjun your mans?" Wass asked. Picota pulled back the machine from my head as if he was giving me space to recall. I glanced in the mirror quick enough to watch him signal for Wass to stop.

"He was—years ago," I laughed.

"Ah! I saw him yesterday with Mariposa coming out of la cabaña."

Essentially, Mariposa spent a whole year traveling back to the Island on every single one of her vacations to parade around El Cibao with Junjun, who she clothed from head to toe, and then the bitch almost married him. Turned family gatherings into war zones over her decision and everything. Her choosing essentially destroyed us. She's never apologized for it. And how can I blame her for being so cold? I would've probably supported her had I not had to hear about it from someone else. Anyway, she was deadass going to bring him over, I heard, until one night, while he was drunk as fuck next to her, she used his thumb to get into his phone.

The morning after we met we went to a waterfall together. Caoba and West Indian cedar trees surrounded the entire place. Marlene wore a bikini and let me borrow a black one-piece she had bought. When we walked into the river, she started speaking to the water. I stood back and decided to give her some space. I watched as she dove in and out of the river, floated, and fluttered her legs.

"You don't like the water?" she asked, standing out of the depths of the water looking like a Ciguapa.

"It's too cold," I answered.

"It has to be. It holds the dead."

"What?" I said. Confused as hell, but frankly a little drunk from the beauty of the place and her. She held out her hand. When we stood side by side, the water slowly dancing around our hips, she repeated again, "It holds the dead. So many of our ancestors were drowned in these rivers," she said. "Look."

The rocks morphed into the faces of elders, adolescents, and children at the bottom of the river. I pulled myself from her fingers. That was when I first started to learn when it was safe to hold her hand.

"Don't be scared," she laughed. "It's a gift, or at least that's what my grandmother says."

It took a while for Marlene and me to connect again. You see, being on the Island isn't the same thing as being in the U.S. It's like the Caribbean water has a heartbeat for dreams and the Atlantic swallows it.

"Here's the thing—" Marlene started over text. I stared at the ellipsis like the world I had let myself get comfortable with was about to give me clues how to fix it. "I like you. Pero my grandfather just died. My family is a hot mess. I lost my whole damn job. I don't want to start something from this place right now."

I agreed.

And then three months later, on a day when the snow was falling like hair clumps, we saw each other on the train.

A vibe since.

We arrive at the family home mid-afternoon. There are hugs and kisses and passing of the children. Bendiciones rain all over the place. Our grandfather built this house from the ground up himself. Had all of his kids living in a shack out back until it was ready. Designed it knowing he wanted a long line of descendants. Seven bedrooms and four bathrooms. And we make it small in a matter of seconds.

The dembow gets loud. Four women from el callejón come through and they hold a bunch of us between their legs, braiding our hair. The empty emerald bottles of Presidente are transferred to the backyard as quickly as the ones vestidas de novias are delivered from el colmado.

When Toño Rosario comes on, Mami pulls Violet out to dance. And I laugh at the growth we've made. Violet's hips weren't always this loose. Mami's mind wasn't always this free. Mami whispers into Violet's ear, and they look at me and smile playfully.

"What is it, you weirdos?" I laugh.

"Marlene!" Mariposa calls from Mama's bedroom. She hasn't said my name in years, and I roll my eyes as I move toward the space she takes up. All the joy I was experiencing vanishes. I feel myself whirl into anger as I get up from the chair. Violet touches my back with a free hand as I pass by her—*Bring it in. Don't give away your power.*

Mama's head is hanging off the bed, while the rest of her body clenches to it.

"She won't let me take her to the bathroom. Keeps asking for you," she says. Annoyance crawls up my throat like a scorpion.

"She don't know you." I put Mama's arm around my neck.

"She was trying to force me," Mama whispers. She cups her other hand on my shoulder. It would be easier to carry her, but she doesn't like that.

"It's Mariposa. Marandrea's firstborn," I say. Mama glares at me like I've dropped a bomb. I continue moving her toward the bathroom.

"I didn't see the ocean until I was almost thirty, but I always felt its waves. El Mar is even in my name. That's why I made sure it was part of my children's names. I wanted them to feel it too, to expand forever like it. But I didn't want that name, dique Marandrea," Mama says.

"Tu abuelo became infatuated with a woman of poder en La Capital. Her name was Andrea," she begins. I bite my tongue. Mama has taken to telling the truth lately. The dementia becomes a twisted gift because now she can finally tell the narratives that have rusted inside of her for so long.

"Mama, you don't have to say anything," Mariposa says from the door. I sit Mama down on the toilet. Only when she's comfortably sitting do I turn to Mariposa.

"You don't get to tell her when to be quiet. You can go now," I say.

"Excuse me?"

"That mujer. She had her family. Her político husband. She could've left us alone. Before I knew about them, I thought I was lucky. To be the only one of my sisters and comadres without a cheating husband. But he was just like every man I knew. A good wife wasn't enough. He wanted me to stop teaching when we married; I did. I wanted three kids, but he wanted more. I gave him seven. He didn't want to see me bored as a housewife at home. I made a name for myself, organized for the sick and needy, forced the thieves we call politicians to pave the roads in this pueblo. He didn't want me to spend too much money, so I never touched it without his say-so even when my children needed it, mi'ja. I was elegant, a woman of God, a woman of my word. I showed up for him, always. Marlene, I gave him so many chances. So many. As leona as I was, that man turned me into another one of his cattle. Cured me just to poison me again, time after time. And I stood. Just because I loved him. Just because I loved him too much."

"Mama—"

"Shut the fuck up!" I whisper through my teeth at Mariposa.

"I'm happy you love women, Marlene," Mama says, tapping the top of my hand. "Only we know how to love each other in full. Sin relajo." I shake my head playfully at her. And we stay like that for a while, smiling at each other, her brown eyes gray at the edges, but still shining.

"What if I love a man?" Mariposa asks, out of nowhere, cause no one was talking to her really.

"Then you pray." Mama takes a bit of paper and cleans herself. "You pray he loves you more than you love him." She flushes the toilet and stands on her own two feet.

Strong. Firm. A woman of her word, expansive like the ocean.

Since I was a small girl, I've slept beside my grandmother even on the days when my grandfather returned from el campo. She always saved me a crook underneath her arm. And since he passed, I've slept beside her whenever I visit. All that to say: I know how my grandmother never sweats in her sleep, and how she snores heavily. What wakes me up is the absence of both the heat and the noise. My eyes flutter open in the dark, but my body won't move. I become dense metal with moving eyeballs. I've had this happen before—watching the spirit world do what it do and being unable to move.

I watch her body struggle in the dark through my peripherals. Witness my grandmother try to catch a breath, her stomach flailing like a dying fish. I watch, behind a curtain of tears, as she attempts to get a final whiff of life, but it isn't granted, and she lets go.

I try to shimmy my way into action, but I remain steel. And so I watch as her spirit detaches from her eighty-eight-year-old vessel and floats up to explore what comes next, straight up into the sky. She touches the moon, gleams at the sun, looks behind the stars for a sign of her God. But then

Mama wills herself to fall back down through the darkness, through the roof, into the house, and onto the middle of the dining room table.

She flows through the crevices of all the bodies inside the home she has sustained for the better part of her life. Every second until dawn, she watches the air mattresses in the living room go flatter and flatter with the weight of kin.

The tears flow out of me and drown the cotton of the pillow below me. Still I cannot move, I cannot wake, I cannot scream. The gravity of the universe presses my bones down to the mattress. I keep my eyes opened—see her see us.

As the sun rises, the darkness of the room is illuminated. Her spirit flows and stands over me, she places her hand on my chest.

You are a dangerous storm, but you're my storm. She presses down, the density of her life plummets into me, and I am pushed back into sleep.

When I am allowed to wake up and move, I rush to touch her face. She's cold. Her brown skin is already going purple. I press my ear to her cold lips; there is no breath. I scream. I shake. I scream. I wail. The door opens. I gather my grandmother's shriveled body into my arms.

What do I do with this, Mama? What do I do?

I thought Marlene was prepared for the inevitable, but she lost it. Lost it, lost it. She turned into a tropical beast. She buried herself in funeral preparations, and any second she wasn't busy, she was rocking her body on Marta's rocking chair like a zombie. I tried to understand it. When I found out Papi died, it was a year after his actual death, four years since I last had seen him, and it still took me a week to get out of bed. It was Mami who coaxed me out by giving me a sobada that nearly erased the pain. I tried to touch her when she cried; at night I would simply attempt to hold her hand but she would push me away. Marlene wouldn't let anyone in, wouldn't let anyone help. I spent most of my days beside her, my hand in my pocket, fingering the ring, and convincing myself she'd say yes—eventually she would say yes.

Today, four days after the funeral, after what seems to be the whole country coming together to put her away, the children of Marta and Pilar call the lawyer for the will. The will was put together by the lawyer la vieja hired four years before the dementia came in swinging, two years after her husband died.

When every family member has found a spot on the galería, the lawyer settles into a rocking chair and takes out a folder from his briefcase. "The totality of all her money, three million pesos, will be split between el lugar de ancianos and three orphanages across El Cibao. The land properties here in el pueblo will be split among her five living children who never sold land behind the family's back. Those were her exact words." The lawyer looks up. I can tell by the look on his face he's expecting a fight, but surprisingly he is met with a collective stillness. "This family home will go to her grandchildren. Her wish is for it not to be sold, for it to stay in the family. If you care about her wishes—again, her words—" He looks around. Mariposa nods at him. "All of the land in Arroyo Torro will go to one person," the lawyer says simply. He looks around at the faces looking back at him as he shuffles through some papers.

"Marlene Vargas."

"¿A quién?" Marlon yells. The comments and questions start pouring in, and the lawyer offers that she was adamant about her decision.

Marlene cackles as she rubs her palms together.

"And what do you know about land?" Marlon yells at Marlene.

"I know not to try to fucking steal it from my dying mother." Marlene stands up on the tips of her feet. "I know how to actually love and care for someone without expecting anything in return!" When the yelling fails to cease, the lawyer makes his way down the driveway unseen. The dark dogs stand up from Marlene's feet and tiptoe around the men—ready.

As the anger subsides, after Marlon tries punching a hole in a wall and instead cuts himself, the silence creeps through the bones of the Vargas family. I hold Marlene's hand, and she lets me. I feel the blood pumping through her, slow like honey, like a thing waiting. Marlon almost falls over as he gets up and walks toward his pasola. The sisters hold the silence the longest. Marandrissa bites the inside of her cheek and looks at her kids with sorrow. I imagine she's thinking, What didn't make them worthy of more of an inheritance? Marilar crosses her arms and looks at Marlene.

"I don't think it's fair, but you and Mama had a special relationship. I know that, but still it isn't fair, and I'm going to tell you right here in front of everyone so that you won't have to hear it from anybody else," she says. Marlene shrugs. The majority of the grandchildren seem to forget that they had claimed the land was worthless more than once in their grandmother's presence. That it was Marlene La Loca who said it was their right to inherit and protect the land their ancestors had gathered up even when they stated they had no desire to live in DR, so why would they want to own anything there?

"So what are we about to do?" Marlenis asks.

"We about to do lo que yo diga!" Marlene yells, her hands smacking up against each other. Everyone's eyes shift toward the corner she is in. She inhales sharply, bringing her afro into a pineapple at the top of her head, and clearing her tears with the backs of her wrists. I wish I had a Xanax or something to bring her down a little bit. They wait on her to speak, to direct the family or maybe to dismiss them, but her gaze becomes distant, as if she hadn't just claimed her power. I tighten my grip around her hand, but it is limp like a thing that is not here or there. I go into my pocket with my free hand and play with the ring. *What is the right amount of time to wait? Would she say no if I still asked on this trip?*

Marlene looks out at the orange skyline as if she is waiting for the answer to fall like a ripened fruit. She lets go of my hand and scratches her head. Clearly her mind is foggy with grief.

I get up to get some water, and come back to sit on the empty chair beside her again. This time, Marlene allows her head to fall heavy on my shoulder, she slips her hand into mine this time, and I squeeze.

The motor scooters and loud cars zoom by. The entire family remains frozen in time. Marlene straightens up again. She crosses her legs and sways in the rocking chair. Her gaze becomes lost again, and suddenly I don't want her to go to whatever place she stepped into a few seconds ago in order to break internally.

"You good?" I whisper, touching her knee. Marlene takes a deep breath and brings herself back, sways in the rocking chair like a rag doll. I look into her eyes. *Are you there?* I see her, and I don't.

"I am feeling the full weight. Right here," she touches her chest and cries, "of becoming my grandmother's second chance."

"You aren't alone, babe," I say, kneeling in front of her. Cause what else can I say? I've only loved elders filled with a burning silence. I don't know what it is like to love an elder who shows you the entirety of who they are. All I know is I don't want Marlene to carry this alone. I don't want to carry life without Marlene.

Prove it, Violet, I hear in my ear. I jolt and fall on my bottom. The cousins behind me laugh a little bit, and Marlene, tears still rolling down her eyes, bites her lower lip to keep from joining in.

I gather myself up and kneel. I reach into my pocket. I pull out the ring. I saved two years for this. An oval-shaped diamond sapphire that resembles the waters on a white gold band. Those closest to us gasp.

"Oh my god! Oh my god! Where's my phone? Record this!" someone screams. The red in Marlene's eyes clears a little, and I don't know why, but I know she's back from wherever she was. Inside the brown of her eyes, a glimpse of herself appears through the layers of grief.

"I had a speech, my love," I begin. "I had a plan to do this in front of Mama Marta and your entire family. And then I was going to wait until this was all over. But I want to show you that I mean it when I say I'm here for still waters, I'm here for high winds, I'm here for the flooding. I want to always be here. With you, Hurricane Marlene. Will you marry me?" Marlene nods, the bags under her eyes stretching with her smile.

I reach out and take her hand. Begin placing the ring onto her finger. When I look up at her, I am stunned when I see the vieja's face behind hers. And another one behind hers. I fall back onto my ass again, the ring dangles from the middle of her finger. I quickly look around, making sure not to cause too much more of a scene, but nobody else is seeing this but me. I observe the eternal line of faces behind one another: folks, men, women, kids, people resembling one another and not resembling each other at all. I blink, take a deep breath, and stand up. Marlene stands up too, and I swallow as the faces remain behind her. Marpilar smiles from the corner, tears coming down her face. I focus on Marlene's face, and everyone on this side and the other blurs. I push the ring onto her finger. A perfect fit. I take her into my arms, bring her up into the air. And although she hasn't changed at all, she is heavier than she has ever been.

We Never Did This to Be Beautiful

ARIANA BROWN

we've picked a color to make her happy / honey blonde or burgundy /
a hollering red / blissful obsidian / a dreamy lavender / after the wash
& waking / of each strand / with something to keep moisture / I touch
the scalp with ease / bring only good gifts / & listen to the singing
in my lower back / neck / arms & wrist / when I conjure the souls of
these digits / to practice / my pinky gives me the most pain / when
I am braiding / shouts at its bend / ties yarn or kanekalon / at the
square root of someone's head / someone who I love / & my shoulders
hunch in defiance / & my forehead oils itself anew / & my knees bring
their grievances / to the top of the bloodstream / & here / is my body
/ wilting in reverence. / if I could / I would destroy every memory /
of standing in a mirror / with brush & head half done / the feeling of
needing help / & no one to ask for it / I don't know what the world
expects / of little Black girls but / it isn't / freedom / to know oneself
intimately / to take pleasure in our many transformations / grow 18
inches of weave in the span of a few hours / & be recognizable only to
those who love us whole / & consistently / I make braids or conversation / & the head I am working leans & aches / we cue a movie / coo a
humble song / & ours is a texture architectural / mimicking the forest
& its triumphant green / I take the shape of trees / I am as old as the
unshed leaf / every spruce cedar & pine is showing off for me / & all
my sisters deserve the sun's reach / the wind's kiss & howl / atop the
scalp / proof we are the earth's earliest kin / shapeshifting for protection / & when we are done / I slip each end through a candle's light /
or cloth and burning water / a small flame prayer / sent up in smoke
/ or sealed & soaking / in the center of my hands / this I learned / this
I taught myself / a secret I pass to all I love who mirror me / I don't
know what the world expects / of little Black girls but / we never did
this to be beautiful / though we did become so / in the process

For the Black Kids in My 8th-Grade Spanish Class

ARIANA BROWN

For Eddie, T, Alexis, Michelle—
island at the center of the room,
dark utopia in the middle of middle school.

When the girls I was friends with in 6th grade
started bullying me in 8th grade, I stopped
talking to them. In retaliation, they shoved me
in the halls, pushed my books out of my hands,
and talked shit. Loud. In class.
For everyone to hear. Worst of all,
they made fun of my Spanish.
So I drifted to sit with the Black kids
and it was there, in the classroom
of Señora Quiñones, the four desks
in the middle of the room, I could unveil
my whole self without shame.

For the group of people who helped me
find my natural rhythm, who taught me
to trust it, to be Black and laugh
with my whole body.
For Alexis and Michelle, who laughed
and showed every tooth, every time,
who dragged joy from their lungs
and threw their happiness in the air.
When they reached you,
you couldn't help but catch on
and make the happy sounds too.
For T, who chuckled at my jokes

and wrote the lyrics to "Roses"
by Kanye West in my notebook
so I would fall in love with hip-hop too.
And for Eddie, the quiet brother
taking notes in the back, who once shouted
Where the hell is my pinche cuaderno?
so loud, all us Black kids shouted,
then laughed 'til tears poured
out like music notes and there
we were, filling the space with the sound
of us again.
The descendants of slaves
have always been the kindest to me.
Eddie and I were the only ones
good at Spanish. The others
were good at being free.
Blackness, the gift my father gave
me, is the most human thing I have
ever been blessed to be. Bond
that cannot be broken should we choose
it over supremacy.

I have never needed a country
to love me—just Black people.
I have never needed heaven—
just Black people. Eddie, Alexis,
Michelle, T—you gave me permission
to love being Black. Who taught you
to love the texture of your hair
and the color of your skin?
The shape of your nose and
the shape of your lips? Who taught you
to love yourself from the top of your head
to the soles of your feet?
Who taught you to love your own kind,
the race that you belong to, so much so
that you only wanna be around each other?
To be what God gave you—beautiful
'cause we chose to be, together

'cause we're better that way.
When I tell you no one in the world
makes me laugh like Black people,
makes me love like Black people,
I mean it's the first thing people notice
about me. It's the first prayer I wake to
and the longest song I am grateful to sing.
Should I ever be shamed inward
for wearing a dark cloud on my head,
should I ever think myself better
for being a lighter color, let me remember
the dark utopia from whence I come.
Should I ever forget that Black people
have demonstrated the greatest acts
of humanity, of courage, that we are
no one's second choice, that no matter
where they put us on a map,
we will find each other—
create our own worlds—
and they will be enough.
Let us be enough.

Lido's Day

YAMILETTE VIZCAÍNO RIVERA

YULIZEDA WAS sure of only two things: that she had to leave Loíza, and that everyone would try to stop her.

Two days of the ringing in Yuli's head had sealed the deal. She leaned against the doorway of her mother's turquoise shed, in the direct line of the jumbo fan, and squinted as she mulled over the thought. The brightness of the midday sun was dialed all the way up, its humid heat bending the sight of overgrown weeds in the yard into waves. The afternoon rain felt far off, but yesterday's still hung in the air, a promise as heavy as a hand on the shoulder. Yuli blinked her eyes closed and shook her head to dispel the ringing. When she opened them, Saff had appeared in the driveway.

Yuli surprised herself with her own sound of relief as her oldest friend grinned at her from underneath a mop of dark curls. She couldn't help her smile as she took in the contrast of Saff's dark-wash jeans with her usual crisp black-and-white polka-dot button-up, trying not to think about her own worn T-shirt and painting shorts.

"Hola, Señorita," Saff said as she approached, pointing to a stray yellow pamphlet at Yuli's feet, emblazoned with "Channeling = Together Forever / Canalización = Unidad Eterna" in dark lettering. "I see you already have the literature. Have you considered connecting with your loved ones from beyond—"

Yuli sucked her teeth to cut Saff off and turned, stepping over the pamphlet into the shed. "Tu sí eres especial—you know you're not funny, right? You're starting to sound *just like* those pendejos, it's terrifying," she called over her shoulder, unstacking a second plastic lawn chair.

"I do know, actually. The better question is: *you* know you can lighten up, right?" Saff countered, also stepping over the pamphlet and lowering her head to clear the doorway.

"Or maybe it's that you're just not as charming when you're late."

Saff settled into her chair, propping up her legs on a storage box in an attempt to leave some space in the now-crowded shed.

"Por favor, you're literally still wearing your bonnet," Saff laughed.

"If you had this headache, you'd get why I'm not messing with my hair today," Yuli grumbled, turning to the precariously balanced open suitcase and pursing her lips at its haphazard contents.

"If I had that head of hair, I'd never cover it up," Saff said, but when Yuli turned to assess her expression, Saff was already leaning back in the chair, looking out the window with her hands laced behind her head.

For a moment, Yuli stared out the shed's small window and let the increasingly piercing pain behind her eyes have its way. She withheld the thought *"easy for you to say"* because she knew, after the years spent in this shed with Saff, how it would sound: half pining, half whining. Because *everything*, down to the effortless glint of the midday sun off of her watch, was easy for Saff. This was why, despite the way Saff's presence smoothed the frayed edges of Yuli's anxiety, she was still unsure of why she'd invited her. Saff wasn't more likely to like this plan than Mami was . . .

"So when are you gonna tell me our super secret mission?" Saff interrupted.

Yuli tamped down the pang of guilt as she imagined phrasing her request in a way that wouldn't let on to the truth: Yuli would not only be requesting a ride to the airport, she'd also be leaving Saff to tell Mami that she had no intention of returning. Yuli reached a shaking hand to pull the end of a worn forest-green blanket into the suitcase, but misjudged and bumped the case so hard it started to tip away from her. Saff dropped her legs and moved quickly to help, but Yuli had already stabilized it, and their arms ended up in an awkward half embrace. For a beat, their faces hovered close enough to one another that Yuli could smell Saff's soap—eucalyptus.

"When," Saff murmured after a breath, "are you going to tell me what's wrong?"

Saff's touch was like an ocean breeze, but Yuli still yanked her arms away and crossed them over her chest. She turned toward the tiny window again. The wood paneling of the shed was already losing its turquoise coat from last year in large curling flakes. The lime-green trim wasn't faring any better, and this piqued a familiar rage in Yuli. It wasn't even a window—hell, the shed wasn't even a shed. Her old rage broke through again: *Why do we do this—why can't we just call things by their names?*

"This was an outhouse," Yuli said, and Saff narrowed her eyes and crossed her own arms at the tone.

"Okay? ¿Y . . . ?"

Yuli turned to look at her then, and Saff's eyebrows shot up.

"You're . . . *crying*?" Saff asked.

Yuli pressed on.

"This was an *outhouse*. Not a shed. That's why it's so far from the house. Mami doesn't know you're here—never knows you're here, actually."

"Are you saying she wouldn't want me here? I thought you said she never even—"

"*No.* That's not the point. The point is people used to come out here, pop a squat, and *take a dump*, and even though I know that, even though I know we all know that, I have to call it a shed, 'el cobertizo,' 'la casita allá 'tras.' It makes *no sense.*"

"Yuli, nena, I . . ." Saff put her arms out in a helpless gesture that mirrored the pleading in her eyes.

Pressure built in Yuli's head, and she told herself it was the humidity, the afternoon rain announcing that it would be coming soon. She squeezed her eyes shut.

"Has it really never happened for you?" Yuli asked, knowing she was badgering and being unfair, but still unable to help herself.

Saff's eyes flickered to the edge of the forest-green woven blanket that was still dangling out of the suitcase before saying, "This is about your brother, isn't it?"

"Just answer, please," Yuli whispered.

"How's your head?" Saff pressed.

"Saff—answer me."

Saff shook her head and drew in a deep breath. "I've told you a million times, Yuli, no. It never happened for me. It doesn't happen for everyone."

Yuli nodded at the familiar lecture. By now everyone knew the basics of how the Channeling worked, it hadn't been news since the First Experience, almost fifty years ago. That the dead could come into any mind that was solitary enough, focused enough, and inviting enough was as much a fact of life as the hum of Coqui's song. *Could* being the operative word. Just because they could didn't mean that they would. There were exceptions.

"Like me." Yuli finished her thought aloud. "It's not going to happen for me either, I don't *want*—" But the pulsing behind her eyes intensified so much that it forced her eyes shut and stole her breath away.

"Yuli . . . how long have you had this headache?" Saff pressed.

"You know what? I changed my mind; you need to leave."

"I swear I will if you want me to. But first you need to tell me that everything is going to be okay when I go. Does Leida know?"

Yuli barked a laugh. "Mami is the *last* person I would tell."

Saff sat on the ground, deflated. "You think it's him?"

Yuli sank to her knees and let the tears come in earnest then. Of course it was him. From the moment Leida had begun preparation for Lido's Day, Yuli had been unable to keep her dread at bay. Again they would mourn her older brother's passing more than twenty years after the fact. Once again they would obsessively set up a million small items pointlessly around the house, sit in separate, silent rooms, and wait for a spirit Yuli had never met to come visit. It was pointless; it was infuriating.

The intensity of the obsession seemed to Yuli to be endemic to the area. Only in Loíza did that tone that made Yuli's teeth grind together come into people's voices when they spoke of it. That Yuli had seen no real evidence of the fact in all nineteen years of her life did not seem to matter: Loíza was considered the point of origin of Channeling. People around the world acknowledged it as such, often making pilgrimages to meet the Original Illuminators, to ask them for guidance on how to connect with loved ones and ancestors. Only *here* did Channeling seem to be the blood coursing through the veins of society, inspiring more fanatical extremism every day. What made matters worse was that Yuli had yet to meet anyone else on the island who saw fit to mourn what this culture had replaced. As the history books would tell it, there had once been music and dancing as vibrant as the loam-and-life smell of the air. Now there was just this hollow thrumming that swallowed everything whole.

"I'm leaving," Yuli finally said, and when she looked up to see Saff's expression, she knew she didn't need to repeat herself. "I can't keep doing this. I can't keep living in this shadow anymore. It's so obsessive here. It's too . . . much."

Saff still hadn't spoken, so Yuli prodded, "What was it like on the mainland?"

Saff blinked.

"New York," Yuli pressed. "When you went, what was it like?"

"Busy," Saff said simply.

"Okay . . . so people lived their lives, you mean? People were *together*? Not sitting as far apart from each other, as silently as they could, in hopes that their brains would be chosen by some random spirit? Not obsessing over how to make sure the renovators don't change too much of *the out-house* because what if your *dead son* wants to come back and can't because the space he knew has changed too much? It's *sick*, Saff!"

She flinched. "Don't say that."

"Fine! Then it's *making me sick.* Can I say that?"

Saff shook her head. "You can, but you're wrong."

Yuli's mouth came all the way open. "*What?*"

"The only thing making you sick is you, Yuli."

The fan blew back Saff's dark curls enough to give a clear view into her eyes. The intense keening in Yuli's ears was starting to pulse, to bleed out into her vision. Nothing looked the way it had earlier. The turquoise wall paint seemed to be reaching outward. The earth felt like it was pushing back against her weight. The air had a sticky quality to it, like it was leaving pieces of itself behind and taking pieces of Yuli with it.

And here we are, Yuli thought. *This is it.* She'd always known there was a reason she never looked Saff in the eye too long, always caught herself if her thoughts started to linger on the way she talked to Yuli without words, the way she handed her things before Yuli asked for them, the way it always felt like one of them was hiding a smile at how perfectly matched they were. Yuli had always suspected that there was a limit to her relationship with Saff, something unknown putting a strain on it. Could this be it? Was Saff really against Yuli's longest-held belief that Channeling could—*would*—only end her?

It was impossible to think through the headache, now reverberating in such an encompassing way that Yuli didn't know how she was still upright, defiantly announcing that whether Yuli liked it or not, her brother's spirit was on its way. But Yuli had always been more stubborn than her circumstances had bargained for. Why change now?

"Get out," she said.

And true to her word, Saff did.

To invite Lido in on his day, Leida had to prepare.

There's no guarantee, she reminded herself between breaths. *There's no guarantee of anything born from love.*

Lido's Day was the only day in the year that Leida needed the Illuminator's platitudes, the only day the honor of waiting lost its shine, rusted into a chore. The box of yellow paper on the kitchen table lay open still, overflowing with Channeling pamphlets and guides from this morning when she'd leafed through them with shaking hands, knowing she would need them.

Leida rose from her seat on the floor to the kitchen window, making sure to take slow steps and slow breaths. She surveyed the short stretch of palmas and flamboyanes between the house and el cobertizo, but before her thoughts could land on who she knew was inside, she made herself return to her seat in the center of the floor.

Leida knew that nothing could force any spirit, least of all a specific one, into her mind, but there were things she could do to help, and on Lido's Day she did them all. When she was done, when there was nothing else left to do, she waited. She drew in breaths, and in between them she looked over her setup again and adjusted it.

She picked up the lighter from the center of the floor and dipped it into the candle as she took stock: the ofrenda that normally stood on a table against the only windowless wall of la sala had been dismantled, with Lido's belongings split between the cardinal directions.

To the east were his images. She was fortunate enough to have many, to be able to run her thumb over the width of his nose, the curl of his lashes. His toys, which there were fewer of, were arranged to the west. His shoes, leather sandals the size of a sand dollar, were to the north. To the south— *breathe, Leida, respira con calma*—to the south, an item was missing.

She had to remind herself—*paciencia, Leida*—that all setups were just adjustments, fine-tuning, something to busy the hands, to lull the mind into a state of calm openness. The only thing the spirits truly needed to Channel was space.

There were no guarantees, but Leida had always been one of the Sensitivas, the way her Mami and Abuela had been before her. Their claim had always been that they were direct descendants of Lola, whose First Experience introduced Loíza and the world to Channeling. Whether or not their claims were true, Leida had learned to listen for signs that something was coming and trust them.

Something was coming this Lido's Day.

It was in the small things, she mused, undeniable shifts in ways that took a hair too long to identify. At that moment, it was something off about the clouds. Just something slightly askew, she thought as she watered the aloe and stared out the open window. The rain smell had intensified predictably, loamy and rich with life, but something about the clouds . . .

Small signs were part and parcel of Leida's life; she would do with just that much information. What wouldn't do was the dread and panic that sometimes came with it. Leida drew in a breath, held it, then let it go slowly, the way the Illuminators taught her: *The center of Channeling is love, the kind of love so deep it strikes you still. Be still to invite it. Respira. Be still to let it fill you. Respira con calma. Be still and use it to reach, and you'll find it reaching back.*

There were those who'd lost their minds waiting, lost their minds to their setups, their adjustments, *their grief.* Leida drew in a breath at the thought, a balm to soothe the slice of fear it always caused. She knew this already. She knew this and held it with ginger fingers, the way she held anything hot, the way she held the knowledge that Lido's blanket was not missing, it was taken. And that there was only one person who could have taken it, a person who was sitting alone in her shed, the way she had been for years. Leida knew that it was her own child, Yulizeda, who had the blanket, just as she knew there could only be one reason Yulizeda had taken it. Leida had always known this reason; it ran through her life like the central reed, the one that all of the leaves could be traced back to:

Leida was going to be left without her children.

The clouds—the thing about them—seemed to be lit from within. For a moment, Leida stared into them and could see herself, rising from her seated position, giving in to the constant pulsing, the magnetism radiating from Yulizeda, that she herself refused to sit with, to take in, to make space for. Leida saw herself going to Yulizeda, breaking her remaining child out of her self-banishment—*why do love and fear hit us hardest when we're alone?*—holding her while she still could, pushing her tenacity back as if it were what grew in overwhelmingly thick coils out of her head instead of hair, demanding that she see, understand.

But she did not. Instead, she drew in a breath. She rubbed a leaf of sage as frail as her love, as thin as Lido's missing blanket—and she adjusted its position on the floor.

Leida would continue to make space. She set the candle down next to the glass of water in front of her, traced the changing shape of its flame with her eyes as it first danced with her breath and then, once far enough away, became a steady, upward reaching.

Leida would make space, and make space, and make space for her babies, even if it didn't bring Lido back to her today, even if it meant Yulizeda would never come back to her at all.

Saff had heard the stories of the Origin from just about every perspective. At first, it would only happen in the middle of the night. And only to folks in Loíza. People would start saying that they were having the most vivid, confusing dreams.

"¡Los sueños más lúcidos!" people gushed at each other, in line at the grocery store, loudly at their tables in restaurants.

It didn't register as a sweeping change at first. Saff knew that this was because the connection through time had always been strong on this spot of the earth. What was one more connection to the past? Still, the shift happened. And then people started coming back glassy-eyed, saying they'd never had a headache like that in their lives. After that, they said, came the visions. "Nunca en mi vida había yo visto algo así," they said, their hushed voices an awe composite, gilded in fear. Once the colors of the otherworldly experience had gripped them, their realities were never the same. And the episodes began to grip almost everyone, one by one, at varying times of day or night, at varying frequencies, but always with the same intensity.

The Channeling seeped into the soil moments after the First Experience and became indistinguishable from any other part of life. Like the sky, ocean, and sand: so clearly distinct from afar, but a search for their separation—fingers digging into the earth in search of the line no drop of salt water can cross—always ends empty-handed.

Saff also knew that Loíza Aldea's particular corner of Borikén—so named after the spirit seen in the First Experience—had its own magic to it. Something else. It was as if that spot of land had its own draw, that corner where the water turned lazily, salty and fresh mingling in a clash with no winner. Time in Loíza bends the sky to land, creating a depression over it much like the center of a lens, dictating a focal point. In this case, a magnetic focal point that draws time back toward it in loops.

Saff's own life had sketched this idea out for her, and watching others' lives play out had only filled in the image, added depth to its color. It gave her limitless comfort to know that this land had always straddled the lines that hold realities together, that it had supported the feet of many before Saff, before Leida, before Yulizeda. It had supported more tensions than the ones that Lido placed on them, and would support many more. This swirl of pain and discovery pushing toward more pain and discovery was nothing more than time opening up once more to swallow those on this spot of land: a memory loop, a question revisited.

It was amusing to Saff to see how Channeling was talked about throughout the world, how people's understanding of it varied not across time, but rather in ripples that went out over earth and water alike, with this corner of land as the epicenter. It was more amusing to see the way this secret told on itself, in the vines looping back in on themselves in the yard, in the corkscrews of hair tersely curling out of Yuli's scalp, in the whispers coming from Leida in the house but being blown back by the wind before they reached the shed.

Being freed of life's limitations had unveiled the world's only true marvel to Saff: the way there could always be, and always had been, a throughline, without there being a line through time at all.

All of this made perfect sense, to Saff at least.

Whether it would make sense to Yuli, Saff knew, was also a question of time. As far as Saff was concerned, it was always a question of time.

The front of the house was butter yellow, bright even against the muted blue of dusk. It was better taken care of than the front of the shed. The door faced the flamboyanes, whose fire-hydrant-red blossoms formed the barrier between them and the river. Because of this, the house was always bright with color, even in shadow.

It had been a long time since Yuli had stood at its front door; she preferred instead to duck into the back door at night after Leida had gone to sleep, and out the same back door in the morning to head to the shed. For so long she had done everything to avoid doing what she was now positive she had to do.

Yuli's head was a boulder. Her throat was raw and pulsing—a wire in the wake of a power surge. And underneath it all was a thrum of anticipation, because she would be using her voice through the pain soon.

She rubbed at the delicately woven deep green threads of Lido's blanket, marveling at its softness. Her head still swam with the vestiges of the colors, with the faint scent of eucalyptus. Nothing looked the same anymore. It was as if the world had shifted on its axis, as if it had been a sketch of some kind before, and now it was a painting, alive with full color, rich shapes, textures that reached back at her as she stared.

She thought she was alone, so it disoriented her when Saff spoke.

"You met him."

Yuli turned to find Saff standing at her side, looking ahead.

"But you didn't speak to him," Saff continued.

It didn't surprise Yuli that Saff knew, that she'd already somehow put it together, that she was already here. Yuli was so used to inviting Saff into her space that she didn't notice she was doing it, how constant it had become. It was amazing how much more sense Saff made to her now.

"I'm sorry," Yuli said.

Saff turned to meet her gaze with a smile. "I know. Don't worry." She extended her hand and the last of the sun's rays reflected briefly into Yuli's eyes with the motion.

"I sent him away," Yuli said.

Saff smiled. "Like you sent me away."

Yuli let out a small laugh. "Just like."

Their hands found each other in silence; Yuli felt the touch like a breeze off the ocean waves.

"How do you feel about going to see somebody with me?" Yuli asked, envisioning Leida inside, kneeling in the middle of her setup, looking up to meet Yuli's eyes, and knowing.

Saff gave her hand a light squeeze. "Of course. Is this about Lido?"

"No," Yuli drew in a shaky breath. "This time, it's about Mami."

Less than a mile of trees away, the river continued to turn its corner into the ocean.

Yulizeda took a step forward.

Manicured Things

SASHA MAHALIA HAWKINS

Somehow I find a blanket of life
and pull it up over my head
I can recall growing inside visions of stories you read
I'm wondering who wrote that book
wonder where they sat down the pain in their head
laying it out like planks of wood
never got treated before they were dead and I remember ripples inside
of your hurt nipples inside of your shirt
I can feel my teeth gliding on rings
all sorts of polished and manicured things I know we wept, we were a
terrace of rice Oh what a terrible price
We paid our dues with a serving of nice I know we kept all of our
feelings on ice thinking that one day I'll open the bottle pour one out
quick for the homies who saw
the look on my face when I held it all soft know they would tell me that
I've gotta stop being hard on myself
Always compelled
to criticize all that I do
and all that I am
is every bit a part of you
       So know that I'm working on loving we too

I'd Always Promised I'd Never Do Drag

DARREL ALEJANDRO HOLNES

You liked me as *straight* as a man
in love with another could ever be,
and I did too. But you also loved
women, how their backs widen
where hips appear, how their necks
swerve like swans swallowing water
when they call your name,
their long hair stroking your face
as they wake from nestling
your chest the morning after.
So here I am wearing the wig I made
in the image of the blondes you preferred
but said you could never love, applying eyeliner
but not for it to run. *I will never*
love him again, I fearlessly announce to the mirror
as I beat my face with powder base into submission,
as if one could ever fall out of the hero's arms and
not back into peril. Tonight,
for the first time, I dance to save myself
from distress, becoming the one woman
you'll never have instead. Tonight, at the Esta Noche bar in
the Mission District, I'm distance. The closest I ever came
to doing drag before was when I was crowned prom king
but chose instead the queen's tiara;
cubic zirconia somehow closer
to real than the king's cardboard cut-out crown.
Tonight, I'm Diamante, extravaganza eleganza,
a gurl singing shine to the Yoncé record,

declaring myself the Queen B of the Night, singing
take all, of me, I just want to be the girl you like, the kind of girl you like
sashay-shantae-strut-shimmy shining on stage,
dunking it like an Oreo, making the masses
shake they asses at the command of
the scepter firmly in my hand. A king,
I queen so hard my earth-quaking rule
breaks the laws of nature; flesh-colored spanx and
control-top leggings tuck it away
where the sun don't shine.
A black lace-up corset covers the missing rib
but lets the rest of me hang out enough to werk
and soak up applause from an audience
who loves this boy dressed as girl,
boy dressed as girly man, boy dressed as man
enough to drag, man dragging on,
man moving on, man gone.

La Negrita

MALIKA AISHA

I laugh at the punchline because I know to.
Everyone is laughing so it's a safe assumption.
People probably know I'm faking.
They probably know I didn't catch what's funny.
Sometimes people stop to explain
but I cut them off before they can finish
so I can tell them *I know. I understand.*
What else can live here if not my grandmother's language?
My Spanish 101 teacher in college was a Spaniard.
He told me not knowing Spanish means
you're not a real Latina.
Despite being Puerto Rican. Ethpañol 101.

I am ashamed. Again, I am made a
growing void without language.

My gramma shouts *mi negrita.*
And when she hugs me, she sways.
It's as if instinct takes her and she
becomes an island. Here there is warmth and waves
and she sways like the trees. I imagine her sitting beneath,
in Salinas, sun blazing and
wind carrying.
Black 101. Once I asked her how to say brown in Spanish.
She shrugged. Said *brówn.*
I failed my Spanish test the next day.
When I came back from Panama,
I said my first Spanish sentence to her.
She stared. Hoped I would repeat myself
until I caught my tongue. She laughed. I blushed.

I am just like her. Cheekbones rounded high
beneath the eyes she gave to my mother, then to me.
Her skin, brówn, like mine. *My twin*, she says.
You don't get it from you mother, you look like me.
Gramma's hands shake now. And she's much smaller.
But her fists still carry. Her laugh still echoes
like she knows something you don't.
Every room is filled with the smell of musk oil.
The one she'd buy off Knickerbocker.
Its scent would linger long after she left a room
and fall into nostalgia like a safety blanket.

Bendición, I say.
Dios te acompañe, she responds
Filling the hole that continues to grow inside me.
Calling me home.

Softness will find you

MALIKA AISHA

On a Thursday morning in Harlem,
an old man walks slowly:
body shaking, hand tightly gripping his cane.
He says,

you know what I say?
ain't nothing on this earth more beautiful
than a Black woman.

How'd he know
I needed saving today?

a letter to my body (the first affirmation is an apology)

MALIKA AISHA

I'm sorry. I don't mean to hurt you.
It is because of you that I understand
ex-lovers; the ones that say they love
you & leave you with scars. I don't
mean to love you this way.
to dig into you, make holes in you,
to watch you as you bleed and still grab
at your skin. You have always deserved
my sincerest apologies. I love you . . . I
try to love you.
Each wound becomes a grave for every
frustration, as well as all the things
I thought I didn't feel. When you
shouted "no," I told you you had to.
So you made a home of yourself, for
men who forgot to leave their shoes at
the door—
leaving tracks all over your skin
and false promises in your pussy.
I allowed you to become an empty thing.
I became just like them—those men
who hurt you. I forced you to collapse
within yourself and attack yourself.
You've been bleeding for so long
and the marks show. No religion nor
church was made of you;
no praise was made for how much
you're made to carry and the deities
of your soul that keep you from

and smile as if i could ever deceive you
when you know every muscle that's
strained.
The house I never allowed you to
make home now creaks; wallpaper
unraveling; every inch of you
caving in on itself with a crumbling
foundation yet I've never tried to fix you,
I just took tools to this body and made
attempts to tear you apart—break away
the imperfections. I poked, prodded,
twisted, and pulled,
believing all that could be torn would
no longer exist. I didn't mean to love
you this way.
Not this torturous, prisoner-in-your-
own-flesh love. Confining you to this
dying thing.
Calling you an embarrassment when
I refuse you your space. When I tuck
and flatten and hold my breath.
I never lend you the space to be
yourself until I can hide you. You have
become all empty promises and no
redemption. Efforts to love you now
feel disingenuous. It's taken too long. It
should not take the pain of my shelter
wearing down for me to lift my hands
to hold you up. I am but a mind while

shattering. Still, you manage to hold without breaking a sweat. There is no amount of apologies that can redeem me. You are tired and every morning we battle.
I call it a small victory while dismissing your needs, dress you to compensate for how ugly I made you feel

you are my earth and my cosmos. Even in your protection, I have not recognized you as myself, only an extension—a temporary encasing. I have done you absolutely no justice and for that I owe you the love that has always been reserved for you but never checked, never announced, never welcomed. All this time I've held it from you assuming that my existence was enough to show you that I love you. That was untrue.

24 de diciembre

IVANOVA VERAS DE JESÚS

Yesterday I dreamed of today,
And today I remember tomorrow. My family is singing and dancin'.
Blissful full-mouthed loud laughs,
Perico Ripiao blasts from the radio. They hug me and serve me food.
Some of them say
They're glad I am here.
They say I am their favorite
niece, daughter, granddaughter, prima. They say I'm the feminine ver-
sion of some random historical "revolutionary." They say I look good
and ask me about "boyfriends."
They say they love me.

Is this when I lose their love?

i think about death all the time (tdor–20 de nov)

SORA FERRI

quiero llegar al punto de mis tías
and look at death as a portal
to a new relationship

Candy and Prey Tell at the hospital:
i tried to create portals for us while you were alive
22 little conversations
of apologies and absolution
promises to be better
ingrain truth deeper
—just to pull the same bullshit and do the whole thing all over
again and again
but deeper every time
but life (lol) doesn't work like that

it's no one's fault
we had communities on our backs, demons on our throats
not to mention each other's own ghosts

but imma keep bugging you
every night, after every meltdown
or when i'm lonely

i'll keep thinking about death—leave my balcony door open
arcana doesn't hold all the cards
we've been ghostly
spooky bitches—backs straight

i learned it all from y'all
i learned to think about death all the time
hasta llegar al punto de mis tías
and monopolize death on my altar
so that finally
my angels and i can throw a fucking ki
—have our fairytale conversations in my living room
princesses
priestesses
all of us looking divine

pride

SORA FERRI

i never never never never never wanted to be trans
not once

no flag or prayer is gonna change that . . . i've tried
and you kno what
i accept this about myself

i'm not even sure if my angels believed in pride
how come my prayers for pride always fell mute?
empty,
awkward.

i don't think my angels believed in "pride" either;
my angels believe in art

finesse
my angels believe in work

in stunting on every body
as we bring food to the table
as we earn you your rights
as we gift you movements
as we gift you generations

have you falling in love with us without you even knowing
the craft

we prove everybody wrong
cackling in our graves
cry laughing on our altars

a craft
that can only be described in prayer

baby me

SORA FERRI

to baby me
who took over when i needed to tap out

    she's 16 dealing with rejection
    she's 16 at a work conference
    her feet hurt
    her stomach is closed up
    she feels moody and impatient
    gets bratty with old white dudes

baby me is depressed
    leaves the office in a fit and trails off on her own
    arms crossed
    she hopes to walk off the burnout
    at least until we can recognize what burnout is
    at least until we can function enough to baby me

baby me loses her man
    she's 16
    she thinks about him all day
    she misses out on a lot and forgets important details

but baby me is capable of so much
    she has felt the worse loneliness and survived
    baby me lost her man so she pouts around all day

wondering what on Earth
will it take for you to baby me.

Home Sweet Homeless

JOSSLYN GLENN

Having just played his numbers for the lottery, a weekly hobby he hopes will go somewhere but which has gone nowhere, Wyclef Arnolds steps out of the local liquor store wheeling his shopping cart of recyclable cans and bottles.

He walks down the street corner on Whittier Boulevard and S. Herbert Street toward Tacos Virginia, a "lucky" routine guaranteed to ensure his chances of winning. With his eye on his receipt, he double-takes at a woman wearing a magician's hat and reclining in a wheelchair, seemingly awaiting the next bus.

Her—those eyes. Are *his* eyes. And as such, he is entranced, possessed into approaching the woman.

"Don't tell me you my brotha Winston," Wyclef manages to say, "'cause he had already gone a mothafuckin' lifetime ago. Sometime after I left for the Marines."

By the grace of her, the woman meekly turns her head up at him with an unmoving pout, a pout likely rehearsed from having played the streets for food, never knowing what her next meal will be and where it will come from. A pout from bus drivers passing her by just by the looks of her, or perhaps she doesn't make it to the bus stop in time and they don't see her. From trying to resist the forces of nature without a shelter to claim as her own to warm, bathe, or comfort her. From being denied by women's shelters for neither passing nor being recognized as a woman in need of assistance.

The pair of eyes Wyclef shares with his newly evolved sister transfix on her backpack featuring Princess Ariel from *The Little Mermaid*, with the name Ariel etched out and replaced with an embroidered "Winona." He had passed by this very type of backpack at a 99 Cents Only Store at several points in his life, though only now does it have significance.

"Winona, huh?" He pauses, hoping she will respond in any way possible. The wink of an eye, a wiggle of her nose, a sound out of the lips she got no doubt from their mother. Nothing.

He continues, "Well, you coming with me then. No sister of mine gonna stay out here on her own, if you feeling me. I ain't lettin' you outta my sight."

Wyclef does not have to say "I love you," nor does he have to question the decisions she made in their period of separation. Wheeling her off is enough. More than any stranger has done to express care for her since she was confined to her wheelchair. All he considers is the fact that both of them are without a home, that in the years they had lost touch, he had not been there to protect her from the injustices that have confined her to a catatonic and immobile state.

If they are going to struggle, they are going to do it together.

What he doesn't know is that his sister has been selling herself on the streets on Washington Boulevard in between Hollywood Boulevard and Crenshaw. Whom she let into her body and how many times she got arrested for "public disturbance," "prostitution," or "false personation" do not come up. While her black eye may be healing, he doesn't need to know how she got it nor by whom. Not that she shows any signs of coughing up answers anytime soon.

By the looks of the sores pierced into her skin and around her mouth, as well as her warm temperature and heavy wheezing, he gathers that she must have HIV and is suffering from lack of treatment. And he is not wrong. No one can access prescription medication or surgeries, let alone a physician's objective, unconditional care, on a sex worker's salary.

Lucky for him, his cart of recyclable materials is full, which means it's payday. This time, the money will not just be his. It will not satisfy only *his* hygiene and withdrawal symptoms, but also those of his long-lost sister.

The measly seven dollars earned can afford a can of beer each and an order off the dollar menu consisting of four tacos, a value drink, and value fries at the Jack in the Box on N. Highland Avenue on the way "home." With the cart empty and folded, they enjoy their 3.6-star meal on the 4 and 720 buses, respectively, so that food coma takes effect by the time they arrive back to Wyclef's alley on S. Atlantic Boulevard.

Once there, Wyclef introduces Winona to his humble abode outside a strip of stores and a particular furniture store frequented by elderly white women who would never have dropped foot in this part of town until recently.

Wyclef unfolds some blankets and a tarp. So as to not lose the wheel-chair, no matter how beaten up it is, he wraps a blanket around her and the back support of the chair. One last blanket for her lap for good measure. For him, a cardboard bed and scraps. No "lights out," though, as lampposts don't turn off until 6:38 a.m. Every time.

While not as busy as rush hour, the street still hosts a moderate number of cars that will, in no time, enter one ear and exit the next. A pure ASMR lullaby interrupted in the middle of the night by muffled moans. Contained, but enough to wake up Winona's light sleeper of a brother.

"You don't talk, but you sure as hell rub one out like a motherfuckin' running motor over there," Wyclef mutters through his drowsiness. But after stretching and rubbing his eyes, he doesn't so much catch Winona as the tall, lanky man thrusting in and out of her.

She just lies there, like a sex doll, slouched against her wheelchair, from which she was likely dragged out. Motionless, inaudibly breathing, seem-ingly lifeless. As this lanky man thrusts in and out of her body bolted to the ground.

The man's Adam's apple, among other body parts, suddenly meets none other than Wyclef's fists. He goes without words, speaking only with his fists. The only audible tone in the alley comes from the man's shrieks, his gasps for air drowned out by a series of cars passing by a long green traffic light.

With one final kick, the lanky figure trips over himself to flee out of the alley. The anger still present, Wyclef turns it toward Winona. "C'mon, make a noise! Any noise! Say ANYTHING!"

But alas, silence. Even in the dark, even on her dark melanin skin, the bruises on her upper thighs and shoulders glow. It's hopeless. He recog-nizes that it's not her that he's mad at. *If I can't be there to keep her safe when she's right next to me, can I do anything to protect her?*

He does not waste a moment in apologizing to his sister as soon as she wakes up. He did not sleep last night; he spent the remainder of the night pondering a number of ways to make up for projecting his frustrations on her and not protecting her . . . again.

"Imma take you to this salon, then the beach . . . oh wait, the salon after the beach so we don't fuck up that 'do. I know this one bitch at this one salon on East 85th Street—or was it 88th Street—that I used to bust into when I had the Bentley. Remember that?" Wyclef stops to realize that his sister has no semblance of the type of relationship he has with his brothas to even know what he is talking about. "They *caribeños como nosotros*[1] and they can get you a fine press or extensions or a highlight," he pauses, "you know, like Mom."

His sister turns her head at him. With just the purse of her lips, it's almost as if she is incredulously telling him, *Yeah right, and with what money?*

"I'll show you." Wyclef smirks.

"Mama and Pops took us to the beach once. Remember that?"

Winona remembers the drive out west, a place her eyes had the privilege of gazing upon only during the summertime. A part of town adorned with palm trees, fancy cars, and shopping centers she only dreamed of sifting through and carelessly spending money at.

She remembers the sand-castle set her mom found for her at an estate sale, the wireless boombox her father used to play his favorite bachata and reggaetón hits. But she could never forget what happened immediately after. And pretty soon Wyclef remembers too.

"Sorry . . ." His voice trails off.

Could she ever forget that she never got to use that sand-castle set or dance to her father's music because soon after arriving at the beach, her father whooped her ass upon discovering that she had hidden a two-piece swimsuit she had stolen from a more affluent childhood friend under her T-shirt and trunks?

She remembers talking back, after which her mother shouted at her in a thick Belizean accent, "Are yuh the mom aw am ah? Do ah look like your best friend?" Translation: Don't patronize me. Don't talk back to me. Know your role. Her eyes did not once divert from Winona's every movement.

Her father forcibly removed her bikini top that indented her skin as he shouted, "*Carajito, te pasaste. ¿Por qué me haces coger un pique siempre?*"[2] (Dominicans pull out an intense, threatening, and rapid burst of Spanish that stings before any beating can.)

---

1. "Caribbean people like us."
2. "Little boy, you crossed the line. Why do you keep pissing me off?"

She had no choice as he shoved her to the ground, pulling down her trunks to reveal the bottom half of the bikini.

"Bend over," he demanded, which prompted her to wince in anticipatory familiarity before his hands struck her bottom.

He thereafter stripped the bottom half of her bikini, revealing her bare ass and penis to beachgoers in their vicinity, who did not once intervene. Winona held her tears as she did her crotch so as to not give power to those who had witnessed her public humiliation. She noticed parents warning their children what kids like her deserve for being subversive. Some kids winced, while some adults did not bat an eye and simply turned away. Not their problem.

As if her father's *tabanas*[3] were not enough, her mother came in on the action by removing her sandy *chancleta* and whacking Winona until she finished shaking off all the sand and packing up all of their belongings. Despite a *whoosh* here and a swing there, she got off easy because *at least they left the belt at home*, she thought.

On the way back to the car, her father shrieked, "*Si sigues jodiendo te voy a dar un cocotazo en la cabeza.*"[4]

Her mother chimed in with, "Yuh—ah en able. Doh have no behavior, man. Doh digging ah horrors!" (You are too much. Stop misbehaving. Don't get emotional!)

As a sex worker, Winona had never felt so exposed. She never returned to the beach . . . not with her family, not with her *panas*,[5] not even by herself. Not at all. Not . . . until now.

Here, on a stained white towel atop the warm sand at the beach with Wyclef, Winona recalls her younger self returning home to a comforting top bunk in a room she shared with her younger brother, who looked up to her figuratively and literally.

"*Tumba eso*," let it go, he said.

She cannot forget how, in so few words, her brother defended their parents and exemplified a manner in which many men have treated her in her life since then. That was the first time she saw her younger brother as a boy. A boy destined to be a man, and all the toxicity that carried with it.

---

3. Manner of hitting with one's hands.
4. "If you keep fucking around, I am going to bust you upside the head."
5. Dominican slang for "friends."

Winona turns to a shirtless, more sensitive Wyclef—he basking in the rays from the sun, she basking in the thought, *¿Por qué sigo metiendo la pata?*[6]

Not just that one time at the beach did she think that, but months prior when she ended up at the wrong place at the wrong time.

Why did I enter his car? I told myself I was done for the day. I was going to grab doughnuts with the girls on the block. I got bruises instead. Filled with blood, not jelly. He took all the money I made that night. He took my voice. But just like with Mom and Pops, I didn't go without a fight. I didn't just take it because if I did, well, hell, I wouldn't be here. With my brother.

"I must've come to this very spot dozens of times," Wyclef says, adding to the ambience of indistinct chatter, seagulls, and waves around them. "Usually at night, though. Usually all by my lonesome. Good to have you here, sis. You're not alone."

I am not alone.

"Let's get out of here," her brother says.

So they go to the salon, as Wyclef promised. And they manage to get a generous discount thanks to Wyclef's flirtatiously charismatic aura, which charms the stylists and wins back that one stylist he mentioned sleeping with. Oh, and their financial circumstances (or lack thereof) make for a great excuse. Apparently, they frequently serve homeless people on the weekends.

No one had quite seen such a smile on Winona's face, which glows as rarely as crisp blood-orange leaves grow and fall during autumn time in L.A. On the way to Mar's Caribbean Gardens Belizean restaurant in Gardena, which was suggested to them by a Belizean client they met at the salon, who said that the restaurant serves "authentic Caribbean food made by actual Caribbean people," Winona's smile stops Wyclef in his tracks when it disappears.

"What happened?"

Wyclef must have forgotten she is mute. The only indication of what she is thinking comes from her gestures, no matter how small. And right now, she stares straight upward at the sign of the establishment right in front of them. It reads: Bienestar. The logo contains a trapezoidal mountain of stairs going upward, all superimposed over a swirly patterned design. "What of it, though?"

He pulls Winona's wheelchair to the side window to check out a flyer taped to the inside of the window. Bienestar is a human services organization that seeks to provide community health to Latinx LGBTQ+ folks, from

---

6. "Why do I keep messing up?"

mental health counseling to resources on substance abuse and AIDS/HIV prevention. It offers case management, a food bank, sexual health education, and housing assistance.

Winona had heard about the organization from fellow girls on the block, but she never had the gumption to go in on her own. With her brother by her side, she has the strength to go in and hopefully get some assistance with her trauma-related catatonia and AIDS-related complications, as well as assistance with legally changing her name and gender, and access to gender-affirming businesses.

Wyclef sees that they aren't operating right now. He does not have a phone to check the time, so they will get there when they get there.

"We'll come back in the morning. How 'bout that?" Wyclef offers.

Winona turns to him. Wyclef can see that glow again. Such hope and optimism in that glow. It can't be too good to be true.

In the meantime, he treats her to authentic Caribbean food with money he has been carrying around just in case, and for a moment, he feels he has absolved himself of the guilt of not protecting her last night and all these years. But on the Metro back "home" . . . "Nigga, is that your bitch?"

Wyclef ignores the passing comment, hoping the man will keep to himself and leave Winona on a high note just until the buses start running again the next morning. But, of course, he cannot control or predict the stranger's actions and knows men like him—drunk or otherwise—grow aggravated and defensive like his sister being trans is personal to them.

"You ain't say nuttin'. Sorry to tell you, but, son, you guilty. What you like about trannies that you don't get from a real woman, huh? Don't tell me. You stroke it, suck it off? You like that, nigga, don'tcha? Guys," he says, turning to his entourage, "this nigga is all about bendin' over to have trannies busting a nut inside him."

The man riles up his peers in a frenzy.

"Nah, he ain't nuttin' but a tranny-fuckin' fag, guys. I don' got no problem wit you tryna nut but I bet you suck him dry wit dat mouth, huh? You don' gotta marry da bitch, take him around town like he some trophy prize. You gotta tell me, 'cause I just don't understand. You really gotta break it down for me."

Wyclef grinds at the teeth, or what's left of them, aggravating the prominent vein on the left profile of his forehead. Bruxism has left his mouth victim to fractured and chipped teeth, jaw soreness, and even some tooth loss. He is not worried about these men misperceiving his relationship with Winona. He is worried that no matter what, he cannot guarantee Winona's safety even if he tries, because her inability to pass will keep clocking her and threatening the personal sensitivities of others. All he has to do is wait until tomorrow and everything will be all right. Winona will get the necessary care to recover. That's all. It will be as if he made up for lost time. But time cannot heal past wounds in just one evening.

That said, he whispers to his sister to cover her ears and close her eyes and think about what a great time they had today. He tells her, "What I'm about to do now does not deserve to be a bad memory clouding such a beautiful day."

Before they know it, they have returned to their layers of tarp and scraps scrunched against a cool limestone wall on S. Atlantic Blvd in Montebello. Blocking out the sound of scurrying rats, dripping pipes, and rank garbage bins. The pair have known this to be true for over a decade now living on the streets, although around different parts of the city. In fear of losing the wheelchair to some klepto fiend, he locks her brakes and lies down, arms resting beneath his head and neck.

With one blink, he is out like a light. In the next, he is up again, hands throbbing and head aching. No concept of time to indicate how long he has been out. This leaves him in a panic that quickly draws his gaze to Winona. Where is Winona? Street lights neither gleam nor peek into alleys, so this brief state of frenzy ends with a slouching and thankfully breathing Winona just inches from him. Ariel the mermaid is still smiling, and Winona's magician's hat has fallen beside her footrest.

How could he possibly relieve himself of this guilt? Would he wake up every day wondering if Winona is still intact and alive? He does not dwell on any answers because before he knows it, he's fast asleep yet again. Until he opens his eyes to an awake Winona people-watching determined passersby in all sorts of professional attire. Maybe, he thinks, she could pull off a white-collar job requiring a dress code of blazers, slacks, and black heels. But he wouldn't even know what she thinks, let alone how she talks. All he knows is that today means a new journey toward wellness: Bienestar.

And to Bienestar they go. Winona could not be any more eager to enter, wheeling herself in almost like a fifth grader walking into class on the first day of school, already confident stepping foot into a space with familiar faces. It does not feel new, but rather comforting. The breeze inside hugs her like a grandma welcoming her grandchild after having just finished baking a warm sweet-potato pie.

Wyclef has business of his own. He typically spends several hours during the day fishing through garbage bins for recyclables, salvageable scraps of food, unfinished drinks, and the occasional ganja or opioids. At this particular bin, on this particular day, he happens upon a shiny artifact. It can't be. Oh, but it is. A six-carat ring embellished with two tiny diamonds on each side of a large, centered diamond, suitable for a wedding.

So he thinks of his sister, and turns to a pawn shop down the road. After all, she could take a while. Furthermore, how is she going to afford treatment for her AIDS symptoms? How is she going to get a California ID? Or any bodily procedures she so chooses? How is she going to live? Live to one day be one of those walking professionals he woke up to this morning?

So he walks out of the pawn shop with brighter days in mind that dim at the sight of two police officers, who not only walk in his direction, but don't stop or turn elsewhere. One officer says, "Excuse me, sir. A woman reported spotting a man with your features stealing a wedding ring."

"If she has a problem, she gon' have to take it up with that pawn shop," Wyclef says, pointing backward. "Is there any reason she couldn't bring this to my attention right to my face and instead enlisted your intervention?"

"Sir, we need to see your ID."

"What for?"

"Sir."

"I don't need to show you no ID. Not here in California."

"You need to cooperate, sir, or else we will have to detain you."

"Shit, what the fuck for? I didn't steal no ring, man. I found it in the fuckin' trash bin on 88th Street. And why you already got your gun out like that? I haven't done nothin' and yet you have your gun out like I got a weapon on me."

"Perhaps she accidentally dropped it in the trash and lost it," one cop suggests.

"Nigga, why you makin' up stories t-t-to protect that woman? Maybe I found it and that's muthafuckin' that. You fuckin' stand around makin' hypothetical stories for her and yet you don't even look at me and hear what actually happened."

One cop gently grabs at Wyclef's wrists. "Put your hands behind your back. And we will see if you have the ring on you."

Wyclef pulls away. "Man, what the fuck! Get off of me! I don't have no muthafuckin' ring on me. Didn't yuh see, I had done pawned it. I didn't steal no ring, okay? I *found* one."

"Get on the ground," one cop says as the other kicks the back of Wyclef's knee in.

176 HOME SWEET HOMELESS

Very soon, another car arrives. Two cops emerge on the premises. He doesn't even remember either of the first two cops calling in extra police, which means they likely felt Wyclef was going to be a threat before anything happened. Which means the person that called the cops saw him and knew he is a Black man.

"Get your hands off me. I ain't done nothing wrong." Wyclef's voice cracks.

"Stop resisting. Sir . . . sir, you're gonna need to . . ."

"Nigga, I served this country. What are even my rights? Huh? Tell me my rights, goddammit!"

"STOP RESISTING! STOP RESISTING!"

Wyclef's arm is twisted, dislocating his shoulder. The four cops pounce on him. There are punches, though he doesn't know from where because he is also being kicked. By whom, he is not sure, because every particle of his body is being stimulated. Triggered. Tased. Ten times worse than getting caught by one's parents for doing something he shouldn't have done. But he didn't. Not this time.

"Get off me, I can't breathe. Nigga, please! I can't breathe! I Can't breathe! I CAn't breathe! I CAN't breathe! I CAN'T breathe! I CAN'T B—"

Two blocks down, an unsuspecting Winona walks out of Bienestar with that radiance again. She wants to share it with the person that got her there. But he is not there as he said he'd be.

What feels like thirty minutes pass before she unleashes the strength to call out, "Wyclef?"

As she turns her wheels around, it becomes increasingly clear that she is all alone.

With Love, from Our Corner of the Night

IRENE VÁZQUEZ

Dearly beloved,

I am writing you a love poem because it is the only thing I am capable of doing. All I have ever asked of the springtime is to bloom again, to be reminded that we are beings worthy of resurrection. It is a truth universally acknowledged that love is a trying thing and it is a truth universally contested that Black life matters.

What I mean is that I am 21, you are 20-something, and Stephanie Washington is 22. What I mean is that we too have tucked our loving into the only corners of the night that will hold us. What I mean is that loving you is a difficult miracle.

At the protest, I do not raise my hands and ask for mercy. How could I, when it is a pair of Black hands just like mine that kept me warm through the winter? I cannot bear re-creating the violence of insisting on my innocence. When we love, they name us insurgency. Call everything our bodies touch looting, including each other. I think I keep asking you for forever because you and I have never been guaranteed tomorrow.

So I text you after midnight even though we haven't been talking. I say, I saw you at the protest and I am drowning in the fact of my Blackness. I say, my poetry professor asked me once to try and find a line that will stick to the abyss, but the only thing that feels solid is the fact of your hand in mine. I say, *come over because I have to write a poem where we are not afraid.*

This is not the poem where I am not afraid. But this is the poem where I love you. Where I hold your name inside my mouth. Where I pronounce every letter. In the face of all this devastating catastrophe, I give you this, my language. I name you, my love, to be my fate.

Dispatches from a Country Without Name

IRENE VÁZQUEZ

I'm not going to make you
leave the poem.

Selfishly, I must admit, part of me clings
to the remains of objectivity,

or at least the subjectivity of a guy with a name
like Walt or William or one of those names

that is all first names. But here you are
in the poem, though I have redacted

your name for privacy.
Redacted, Redacted, Redacted—now I can say it all I want.

If you'd listened you'd know
I only ever promised

difficulty. Haven't you seen
how hard I fight for each poem?

Nothing can be expected from Paris.
All they have given us rots.

You told me once you often think unsummarizable things,
and I didn't know what you meant,

and I loved you for it.
You, my algo diferente.

Once, I dreamed
of a common language.

Somehow, we were most honest
when language split open.

The closest I can offer you
to sense is couplets.

Can't you hear the cicadas
pleading? They too

have loved this mutilated world. All I want
is to wake up next to you again tomorrow.

About You

JESSICA LANAY

AND ANYWAY–HOW would I tell them? My mother prophesying herself grandkids. When my aunt was a cocaine addict maybe she would have said, "Love who loves you," but now as an addict of Jehovah, certainly not. Either way, you don't and won't fit. Your grandmother asks from her wicker-backed chair in her kitchen veneered with raising three children and nine grandchildren if I am your girlfriend. When I don't answer, she insists, "Esa chica vive como si no tiene rumbo!" She isn't wrong. But I can't bear the smell of spring that demands I get my shit together, stuffing colored silk down my throat. I examine the pictures of your grandmother, perfect in her white dress; generations of sepia accomplishment and the color of lemon-oiled wood. Your dead grandfather's smile unsure in his youth, like yours. I can't move forward and I can't go back. My thoughts as persistent as sea foam breaking and burbling—wanting simple things—you prove that loving me back is not simple; it seems natural in the narrative of my life that you would not. Your grandmother tells you, "I like her." Your body my noose. Girlboy, burying your face in my chest in a room full of people and asking, "Where are you going? Why are you leaving?" And it is unfair. Just a palm full of you, a sliced piece of you. Lay cinnamon on my tongue, smack my face, and yank me to knee by my hair. Cleft or compass me. How do I pray to god for you without offense?

Run for High Ground

The humidity soaks through us
at the back door, we look into each other's
faces through the tacked-on screen,
we sag like hand-twisted sheets.

I want to kiss you—you want to rest
on my chest, we are both fearful
of your children's voices, we both know
there are too many but you wanted love
too much to schedule the appointments.

We will never be like our mothers, too hard.
We are too hard, they tell us, our piths
selfish around the sticky net of the parts
that the children and the men want.
Auntie says, *save it for Jehovah.*

But when we feel like it, we part ourselves, flow
like storm water down alleyways, we clot
in the shadows of houses that used to be owned
by our grandmothers; now, no one we know

owns the houses; tourists like flies own them.
When we want to, we rut and smoke menthols
under the sea grape tree, while your son yells
auntie and then mommy, then sinks back into the bed.

Tonight we've waited—the new air conditioner working
we all pile into the bed, limbs like stacked driftwood, five
children all entangled, human yarn around the spools
of our bodies—breathy—little sweats fermenting—a sweet

liquor, their fingers sticky from slices of fresh mango.
You whisper for me not to fall asleep—I lay my head
on your thigh, you play Selena on your broken phone,
we sing in Spanish that sounds like chipped crystal.

We could fall in love, we could fall in love, if life
wasn't already a domesticated macaw on a string.
To help us stay awake, I begin to read poetry out loud
about a woman like us in Paris—you suck your teeth,

you want someone to write a poem about this life,
and in my head already these lines. By now the children
have fallen into the rhythm of sleep, we unravel and creep
through the front door, through the aluminum gate.

We bob away, the embers on cigarettes fading
down the street, we go towards the sloshing sea—
this island like a breadcrumb floating in the open
mouth of some little-g god, ready to swallow.

We can only run as far as the edge, you hate the beach,
I know. But there is nowhere else to go—still five plates
to fill every morning, and when you hold me your arms
are wooden with determination: I know I am never home.

Our feet lathed by high tide, being at the scrim
between land and sea, a stingy dark, is magic
to me, but all you see is blood churning. There
is nowhere else to go, we sit like girls,

in our clothes, at the curling lip of the water
and you do not cry, I am selfish, I cry, but you quake
so deep that you could evaporate into smoke,
you shake so that I bind you with my body

that you don't come undone.

7 Mile Bridge

JESSICA LANAY

THE SEDAN takes the bridge, and my auntie-mommy tells my niece to keep time. Seven miles of concrete ribboned over pylons, connecting the backs of masses that in a storm can disappear. My niece whispers seconds in mississippis; a stone, we skip over the humped vertebrae of sleeping sea beasts of which Cayo Hueso is the head. There used to be a train, but only the pylons in the distance mark its former ingenuity; some abandoned tracks remain. The four-hour drive from Fort Lauderdale: U.S. 1 tapered by ululating water. Every spirit since our apocalypse whispering each name: electricity. New invention creates new problems: my auntie-mommy is terrified of this night drive, wheels bumping over the frailty of what is man-made, the lights that stand like giant metal birds do nothing to brighten the dark wreath of ocean around us. The stacked lights of cruise ships slide by, indicating no distance at all. They will make it down before us. I have elderly family who refuse the bridge, who have never been back across since they first arrived by train.

Come Down

Dream

JESSICA LANAY

WITH HER tongue inside me she hums of floods. I arch my spine in this cool room, handwoven white comforter with plastic pearls sliding to the floor. The window is rectangular and high above my head the sky hovers in powder pink. The sound of a brass waterbug scuttling paper fallen behind the dresser. Her name stuffs my throat: purple bougainvillea hurtling from my mouth like magicians' scarves. I am stupid with desire. The eyeless sea rises, its deafening gallop devours sunlight. In the kitchen, I hear my great-grandmother sing *our God is an awesome God he reigns . . . Lord, Jehovah.* She cooks eggs, the white hens we steal them from cluck. The sea, now one creature, straightens up and holds still; ese o Olokun, for your salt spine. Our windows are made for inundations, we are prepared for storms. She hums hexes inside of me, and I choke thorny bushels—let down, come down. She is doing this better than she has ever done it; licking me to white. Let down, come down. The sea and I lose our spines, now one creature, and in this dream everything is crushed beneath. Only our hair remaining: curly, spiny, floating seaweed.

Sugar

EDGIE AMISIAL

Madame Saint-Ford lived in a mansion, like most of our neighbors. Our community was protected by gates and tall guards with round bellies and menacing eyes. We only left when necessary: for school, work, groceries, piano lessons, and the occasional family vacations. The world was sometimes frightening on the other side of the gates—dirt roads, brown rivers, people in torn clothing, scenes of flames and violent uprisings. Yet it was beautiful, too, with palm trees that stood tall and proud despite the strong winds, despite the silent, palpable pain that lingered above the country like a dark cloud. Our land was a nucleus, an uncompromising allegiance between good and evil, dark and light.

At school, whenever I told my friends that I lived in the Belle-Ville community, I was met with widely different reactions. Disbelief. Impressed nods. Scornful gazes. Living in a gated community in Haiti could mean widely different things. It could mean that I came from a family that hoarded a great amount of generational wealth. It could mean that we worked our way up the ladder and now wanted to separate ourselves from the rest of the city—that we wanted to shut our doors on the poverty, the pain, the noise, and the many other things that frightened or saddened us. It could mean that we were simply people, who lived in a house, within a town, within a city. But nothing was ever that simple. In Haiti, the place in which you rested your head at night was loaded with complexities much heavier than cement, bricks, or stones.

Madame Saint-Ford was my grandmother's best friend, whom she went on Sunday morning walks with. I often went with them, because I was the kind of child who would rather hang out with her grandmother than watch TV. Their conversations were much more entertaining than the translated reruns of *Lizzie McGuire* and *Scooby-Doo*. They spoke about things children should never hear about. Things adults whispered in bed, behind closed doors, while the rest of the world slept. They spoke about their children's terrible husbands, their troubles with menopause, their attraction to the local lawnmowers, and their eerie encounters with Voodoo practitioners.

One morning, they spoke about Farah, Madame Saint-Ford's house-keeper, who had been caught stealing her jewelry a few days before and was fired immediately. She had come back to the house on Saturday night, pleading and begging to be let back in, saying that she had nowhere else to go. But she had already been replaced by Rose, a fourteen-year-old orphan from Cité Soleil—an overcrowded dark town known for violent crimes, gang wars, makeshift tents, and metal homes. I often heard my mother mourn over the large number of chronically ill baby patients coming to her clinic, affected by the diseases of Cité Soleil—tuberculosis, cholera, malaria. When I met Rose, when I compared her thin, frail body to my pudgy belly and developing breasts, when I saw her sunken cheeks and the dark bags under her eyes, I assumed she was sick too—contaminated by a world she never asked to be a part of. I steered clear of her, for a while. I pretended she was invisible. I never spoke to her. I never looked into her eyes, perhaps out of fear, but likely out of guilt. Where did this guilt stem from? I wasn't too sure, then.

Once, she brought us tea after our walk. Madame Saint-Ford spit out her first sip.

"What is this? Poison?" she shouted. "There's no sugar in this. You expect me to drink this? Would *you* drink this?"

Rose apologized and tensed up. Though she stood tall and stiff, she seemed small, like her soul had curled up into itself, hiding from danger. She reminded me of myself, suddenly. Through Rose, I remembered the many times I had reacted like this when being scorned by my parents or teachers. I realized, then, that I had forgotten that Rose was a child, just like me. A child who likely cried in her room after being yelled at. A child who likely wanted to play hide-and-seek with other children. A child who prob-ably hated having to cook and clean up all the time, especially after others.

"Here," Madame Saint-Ford said as she handed the cup to Rose. "Drink it. Tell me how it tastes."

"I will add more, Ma'am," she said, grabbing the cup with her head down. "I didn't realize."

"Drink it," Madame Saint-Ford insisted. She squinted her eyes at Rose, in the same way people usually look at things they are disgusted by, things they hate. Rose was not a thing. Madame Saint-Ford turned to look at me and my grandmother, perhaps expecting us to share her disdain, or to be entertained by the whole scene. Instead, her face fell flat once she noticed my fearful eyes and my grandmother's disapproving pout. I had never seen her be so unkind. She adored children, she adored me. She was the kind of woman who gave kids better gifts than their own parents did—the latest toys shipped straight from America and wrapped in brightly colored paper and satin bows. Rose was the same age as her grandson, whom she loved dearly, and only two years older than me. It was shocking to see how differently she treated us. The tender gleam in her eyes when she spoke to children, when she offered them cookies or tea or books, when she gently patted their heads, was now replaced by inexplicable spite. How fitting, I thought. Madame Saint-Ford was just as bitter as her tea. "Go," she finally said, shooing Rose away with an annoyed wave.

The first time I spoke to Rose, she was bleeding. I walked into Madame Saint-Ford's kitchen to grab a popsicle. Rose was cutting carrots on the counter, her neck bent forward, gaze focused on the task in front of her, elbow rhythmically moving up and down, up and down. She was like a machine. I must have scared her when I opened the freezer. She shouted as the large knife fell to the ground. I raised my eyebrows and glared at her, both confused and annoyed. And then I saw all the blood quickly oozing from her thumb and tainting the clean white tile floor.

"Ew!" I shouted.

"I'm sorry," she said, frantically wrapping a small kitchen towel around her hand. "I didn't hear you coming in." Her voice cracked with every other word. She was crying.

"It's okay," I said, cautiously walking toward her. "*I'm* sorry. I should have said hi or something. I didn't mean to scare you."

She nodded.

"Do you have Band-Aids?" I asked.

"It's okay," she said.

Rose stormed out of the kitchen. Moments later, I heard a door slam. I ran to Madame Saint-Ford and told her what had happened. She was mostly worried about the dirty floor.

"Do you have any Band-Aids?" I asked her. "I think the cut is really bad."

Maybe Madame Saint-Ford didn't hear me. Maybe she didn't want to. She yelled out Jean-Luc's name, her errand runner, her right-hand man— her assistant, basically. But Madame Saint-Ford refused to call her helpers anything other than "*servant*" and "*servante*." She had to remind them, and herself, of the large, invisible gap between her power and theirs. Jean-Luc rushed into the living room almost instantaneously. I always wondered how they managed to hear her calling for them in such a big house.

Despite being over six feet tall, despite his brawny arms and his large hands, when standing in front of Madame Saint-Ford, Jean-Luc seemed small too. He spoke in a soft, low voice and rarely said anything other than "Yes, Madame" and "No, Madame." He had been around since I was born, yet I knew nothing about who he was or where he was from, or whether he had a family somewhere. He reminded me of my father. They must have been around the same age. They shared the same dark brown skin tone, bulky limbs, and scruffy facial hair. It was odd, really. To the naked eye, I looked more related to the housekeepers than to my own grandmother. They were often dark, like me, with coarse hair and brown lips, while the people *in charge*, like Madame Saint-Ford, my grandmother, and the many other elders in the community, were light-skinned with loose curls and pinkish palms.

"Rose left a mess in the kitchen," Madame Saint-Ford said to Jean-Luc. "When you're done with that, go ask Monsieur for cash. Tell him I'm send-ing you to the pharmacy. Get alcohol and Band-Aids." She turned to look at me. "We wouldn't want Rose getting an infection, right?" she said, smiling at me, awaiting my gratitude, as though she was doing me a favor.

Infection. What a dirty word. It reminded me of pus and wounds and ugly things. It reminded me of diseases. Tuberculosis. Cholera. Malaria. It reminded me of Rose, or at least it reminded me of the way I first viewed Rose when I found out where she was from, the way Madame Saint-Ford looked at her when she didn't put enough sugar in her tea.

I was angry, suddenly.

"I'm going with Jean-Luc," I said, quickly getting up to stand next to him. I pushed my shoulders back and held my head up, assuming this would be enough to assert my authority over the two adults sitting in front of me.

"Elsie," my grandma said. "Sit down."

"I want to help."

"We have to go home soon anyway," my grandma argued.

"Jean-Luc can drop me home after." I looked up at him. "Right?"

He cleared his throat and looked straight ahead, clearly avoiding eye contact with me. Madame Saint-Ford glared at him, as if he had done something vile. She rolled her eyes. "You know she loves hanging out with adults, this girl," she said to my grandma. "Let her go."

I knew then that I was good to go. My grandmother never argued with Madame Saint-Ford. Her opinions were the right opinions, her advice was the right advice, always. Maybe because she had a slightly bigger house than us. In our world, this was the unspoken rule—the bigger the house, the bigger the voice. Jean-Luc was a quiet man who only spoke when he was spoken to. So our walk to the store was a silent one, mostly filled with my occasional complaints about the hot air and the seemingly endless path to the neighborhood's gate. By car, it took about five minutes to leave Belle-Ville. By foot, it took about fifteen, which to me, with my short heavy legs, felt like forever. I was happy to be exploring, though. I rarely walked anywhere outside of Belle-Ville, and if I did, I was always accompanied by a family member. But here I was now, on my own in some sense, finally viewing the world that had surrounded me for years, without its beauty being drowned out by my parents' displeased comments about the dirty streets, or the beggars, or the smell of roaming stray dogs and hens.

Out there, everything looked alive. Jean-Luc happily greeted people as we walked down the street—a woman with a basket of fruit on her head, five men playing poker in front of a small church, a man selling sugarcane. Outside of Madame Saint-Ford's home, Jean-Luc was seemingly popular. This surprised me. I had never given much thought to what people's lives looked like beyond the walls of the places I knew. What had I learned that made me expect maids and housekeepers to be friendless beings? Perhaps it had been unfair to believe that their lives solely revolved around us. But who was "us" anyway?

Outside, everyone looked like me. There was no name for the very apparent difference between groups of people in our city. My school, Sacré-Coeur, was one of the most popular private schools in Port-au-Prince, and, judging by my mother's constant complaints about the rising tuition cost, likely one of the most expensive too. Like my neighbors, most of my friends and classmates were light-skinned, with softer hair that was much easier to comb than mine. I had always been the odd one, and my friends occasionally joked about me looking like field workers or mountain men, or basically anyone known to stay in the sun for extended periods of time. There was no name for comments like these, either. I had no way of putting into words the discomfort that these differences made me feel.

At Sacré-Coeur, "us" meant the daughters and granddaughters of well-respected alumni. "Us" meant white button-up tops and gray plaid skirts that covered our knees. "Us" meant the girls who were expected to, one day, make it to America. In Belle-Ville, "us" meant private chauffeurs, gated houses, and oversized backyards. And then, there was *us*—my father, Rose, Jean-Luc, Farah, the "field workers," the "mountain men." There was *us*, and our skin. I could take off the school uniforms, I could leave the gated house. I couldn't get out of my skin—this skin that so vividly made me wonder whether I was living the wrong life.

When we got back to Madame Saint-Ford, I asked Jean-Luc to let me bring the Band-Aids and alcohol to Rose.

"It's three p.m. now, so I don't think she's doing any chores," he said as he handed me the plastic bag. "She'll be in her room. Down that hall. All the way to the back."

Rose's room was bleak and empty, illuminated by a small window the size of a notepad, furnished with only a twin bed and a folding chair. The only piece of decoration on her beige walls was a small photo of her younger self in the arms of a nun.

"Ah!" She winced as I dabbed a drenched Q-tip on her cut.

"I know. This stuff stings. But it helps. You have to let it hurt a little bit if you want it to get better."

"Can I just put water on it?"

"It's too deep. Water isn't going to get all the bacteria."

"Bacteria? . . . How do you know this?"

"I don't know." I shrugged. "I just hear my mom say stuff like that all the time. They don't teach you this stuff in school."

"Hmm."

"What school do you go to?"

"I don't go anymore. I didn't like it."

"Why?"

"The same reason you just said. They don't teach you important stuff."

"What's important stuff?"

"Stuff like this." She pointed at her cut.

She watched as I pulled a Band-Aid out of the box. I peeled off the paper covering with focused eyes, puckered lips, and frowning brows, as if I was solving an intricate puzzle. I carefully placed the Band-Aid on her finger.

"You know . . . It's not bad to not go to school," she continued.

"I didn't say it was."

"I know how to do a lot of stuff. More stuff than other kids."

"Okay."

"I can even change diapers. Can you change diapers?"

"I don't know any babies," I said. "So . . . no."

For a moment, a tense silence lingered between us.

"I'm sorry," she finally said in a low, meek tone. "Thank you."

She bowed her head and slowly pulled her hand away. She made herself stiff and small again, like the many times she had stood in front of Madame Saint-Ford.

There was "us." Elsie and Rose. Two young girls, aged fourteen and twelve, sharing a moment of acquaintance under one roof. One would assume that there was no reason we couldn't become friends. But, as she walked away, I realized that we both knew that the things that made us different held too much weight, took up too much space.

Lulled in the Moment

JENNIFER CASTILLO

"The waking mind with dreams, which may well be
But broken images of the night's treasure,
A timeless world that has no name or measure
And breaks up in the mirrors of the day."
—EXCERPT FROM "SLEEP" BY JORGE LUIS BORGES

The dreams which inundate
my waking mind take me
on a journey
down lovers' lane—the echoes of your giggles,
your cherry-blossom-shaded cheeks flushed,
glaze my eyes over, lulled in the moment.

These residues, yet broken fragments,
of last night's treasure
develop in color in the wells of my heart.

I yearn for a timeless world:
to go unabashedly against the current,
leap into the other's arms,
Time suspended by no measure but our own.
Uneasily affronted by the mirrors of daylight.

Sapphic Ode to Alex Reynolds

JENNIFER CASTILLO

You with ballsy intellect steal my fig heart,
Conquering my quivering pomegranate,
perched high confidently in the grassy shrub.
Blooming fruit devoured.

Lively round eyes irises dark espresso—
Aphrodite blessed you with rosy pink lips,
To calm nervous pacing irrationalities,
Escaping my tongue.

No one warns me: honey-cloaked secrets concoct
The most telling riveting affairs of all,
Surpass shaking knees clad in velvet mist air.
They mark our destiny.
Halsey blares in crashing audio sound waves,
Alas I succeed equal vocal octaves,
Singing like a hummingbird destined to escape,
Ascending to freedom.

Pelo Malo / Pelo Bueno

JENNIFER CASTILLO

I had no recollection of my natural hair texture from birth up til age 8.
Afterwards
all I knew and grew accustomed to
were the strands popping from my head: limp and straight.
What I did remember, from muffled patches of audio from my childhood, were the frustrated grunts of my mother. In the living room, I
sat cross-legged on the floor between her thighs
with my back facing her; my neck bobbed back to front with the tug
from a thin comb. And with
every tug, I wanted for my "pelo malo" to be "pelo bueno."
Next to no
women in my family knew what to do with me: lacking patience,
enthusiasm, and care for my
Hair.

Let me strip down my hair routine bare:
Juana's Beauty Parlor on Claremont—blocked out my Saturday or Sunday mornings, a simple 2 seater hours,

1 hour relaxing, shampooing, conditioning, detangling . . .
Drained on and on . . .
90 minutes under the dryer
30 minutes blowing out my strands pin straight.
But who is it all for?

Justice Served

ZOË GAMELL BROWN

Tonight I cry
For people lost
Lives unlived
Love unfulfilled

I try to think
Of justice fit
For a deficit
So large

An incomprehensible
Depth of destruction
An unfathomable
Amount of pain

I sit soaked in
Cruelty's ability to
Exist, persist
And transform with time

When will we
Truly be free?
And do we know
What freedom means?

tía por qué me dicen q tú no existes–after songs of water saints

FRANCHESCA ARAÚJO

my ancestors transcended time to raise me
moved my vision to blue and yellow beads that held testimonies protected by the sun
she is our oldest truth teller who bore witness to the carving of familial
trees and centuries long community land and water saint worship

while little girls move sensation from burnt ear initiation rituals to
the colorful signals around my neck to natural hair invasion to salon
womanhood lessons

my ancestors' palms transcended time to make jugo de china from all
the curves and spirals of our lands taste of memory and intimacy
of my dad's hands
of burnt coffee grounds during childhood spaces con mamá que me
dice que soy negra aunque ella es color leche

my ancestors transcended land to name me *hija de Ogun rebel carrier
of anger and metal*
le pregunté a tía por qué todos dicen que no existe lo que presenció el
sol
at age three
I ask si fue en esa iguana imperceptible,
on the blue mom crossed que viví
they say yes
and iguanas are sun worshippers
they worship what lets us be complicated

Romo oscuro para Santa Bárbara Africana

FRANCHESCA ARAÚJO

Normally,
We would offer you light liquor

Dark for the men, white for the women

But I know you better than that
Erzulie

When you called to me,
The way it is expected
My dad said
Be careful,
She is jealous and full of rage
Perhaps not a spirit you would like to make promises to
                              It hurt to watch my hero be wrong
But we are tethered
Because you have already claimed us

Boundless lover and protector of girls

Celebrator of intimacy,
Insurgent love and body warmth
Between women

To be so delicate and
Interpreted as vengeful
Occurs when a manipulated culture poisons spirit

To say Black woman caressing the skin of her reflection is fearsome
To say Erzulie, who does it all to ensure our safety, is dangerous

Except I was never scared
She said my ties are stronger to divisiones because of this, not in spite
of

Erotic love of a Black woman
Is shelter
Is going home
To ancestors and
To spirit

Romo oscuro para Santa Bárbara Africana
The color of the skin I kiss with urgency

Electra

ANDREA ALEJANDRO FREIRE F.

Tengo la garganta atravesada por el silencio, aún. Tengo el alma viajera y el cuerpo estático. Tengo los pensamientos cinéticos y el corazón huésped. Tengo, tengo, tengo, hace tanto que tengo y no temo. Ya no temo ser la hija bastarda de la luz, la moradora de la oscuridad. Soy el emperador de la metrópolis torturada. Mi pecho contiene un corazón demasiado pesado y grande para alojarse en sitio distinto de un pecho ensanchado por unos senos. Mi piel y mi cabeza tienen muchos habitantes.

Soy de hierro. Aprieto mis dientes y siento el crujir del hierro. Fui carne y sangre, pero se me agotó la sangre y apareció el hierro. Tanto recuerdo, tanto escape, tanto vejamen, tantos escupitajos me desgastaron la sangre. Temí tanto que comencé a sudar sangre. Mis venas huyeron de su caudal y el río se desbordó. El río de mi sangre se desbordó.

Los vacíos son la cicatriz de una gran herida. La herida supura. El grito se queda atascado en la herida. La herida desaparece. Aparece el vacío. HA MUERTO EL TEMOR.

Electra

ANDREA ALEJANDRO FREIRE F.,
TRANSLATED BY JESSICA LANAY

I have my throat crossed by silence, still. I have a wandering soul and my ecstatic body. I have kinetic thoughts and the heart of hosts. I have, I have, I have—it has been so long that I have not feared. Enough, I do not fear being the bastard daughter of the light, the dark-dweller. I am the empress of the tortured metropolis. My chest contains a heart too large and heavy to lodge itself in the distinct place of a chest widened by its breasts. My skin and my head have many residents.

I am iron. I grind my teeth and feel the creak of iron. I was flesh and blood, but my blood wasted away and the iron appeared. So much memory, so much escape, so much vexation, so much spitting that my blood is worn away. I feared so much that I began to sweat blood. My veins fled their banks and the river overflowed. The river of my blood overflowed.

The empty spaces are the scar from a great wound. The wound weeps pus. The scream stays mired in the wound. The wound disappears. The empty space appears. THE FEAR HAS DIED.

Carne y Espanto

ANDREA ALEJANDRO FREIRE F.

I

La muerte ha vuelto a tener otro orgasmo. Come de mi carne, bebe de mi
sangre. Y el verbo se hizo carne. Y el verbo se hizo silicona. Y el verbo se
hizo lentejuelas. Y el verbo se hizo faja en los pechos.
Y el verbo se hizo carnaval. El carnaval se hizo carne. La carne se hizo
sangre. La sangre es la fiesta líquida de mi cuerpo.

II

Uno puede cambiar de todo pero menos de uno. Uno siempre es uno. No
sé si uno y uno sean dos, lo que sí sé es que uno siempre es uno. Se es uno
y se es otro. Seres duales. Soy un ser doble como un drag king o como un
drag queen, yo no me ajusté a ninguno.

III
Todo lo que
escribo, lo escribo
desde la imposibilidad
de apalabrar mi existencia.
Mi monstruosa, negra
y precaria existencia.

Flesh and Fright

ANDREA ALEJANDRO FREIRE F.,
TRANSLATED BY JESSICA LANAY

I

Death has returned for another orgasm. It eats of my flesh, drinks of my blood. The verb became flesh. And the verb made itself silicone. And the verb made itself sequins. And the verb made itself a bind over my breasts. And the verb made itself carnaval. Carnaval made itself flesh. The flesh made itself blood. The blood is the fluid festival of my body.

II

One can change everything but one. One is always one. I do not know if one and one equals two, what I do know is that one is always one. Self is one and self is another. Dual beings. I am a double being like a drag king or like a drag queen; I do not settle for either.

III

All that I
write, I write
from the impossibility
to speak for my existence.
My monstrous, Black
and precarious existence.

Lx DragOna

ANDREA ALEJANDRO FREIRE F.

Cuando mamá comenzó a inyectarme estrógenos, también comenzó a inyectarme miedo a ser quién soy. Me temí por mucho tiempo. Ahora me abrazo y despedazo de pasión comiendo mis propias entrañas.

Yo, yo soy lo desconocido. Yo soy mi deidad y mi oscuridad. Yo soy unx milagro de carne, carne revoltosa, lúbrica, perversa, violenta. Irreformable.

Monstrux de sexualidad infinita, incansable, inagotable. En mi sexo habita mi monstruosidad.

Sin marcos teóricos ni límites. Solo un cuerpo para devorar.

Lx DragOna

ANDREA ALEJANDRO FREIRE F.,
TRANSLATED BY JESSICA LANAY

When Mama began injecting me with estrogen, she also began to inject me with the fear of being who I am. I feared myself for so long. Now I embrace myself and shatter with passion, eating my very own bowels.

I, I am the unknown. I am my own god and my own darkness. I am a miracle of flesh, unruly flesh, lewd, perverse, violent. Irreformable.

Monstrux of infinite sexuality, inexhaustible. My monstrosity lives in my sex.

With neither the marks of theory nor limits. Just a body to devour.

La reina del virus

ANDREA ALEJANDRO FREIRE F.

tengo el virus / tengo el virus inoculado / tengo el virus inoculado bajo la lengua / tengo la lengua ampollada / tengo la lengua ampollada sobre la mano / tengo la mano rebosante del virus / tengo el sexo lleno de virus / tengo la vida llena de virus / tengo el virus en los ojos / el virus se me escurre por la nariz / tengo el virus en el pelo malo / eu tenho o vírus em minhas palabras / tengo el virus en el torrente sanguíneo / maricón, soy un maricón con la peste rosa / soy un maricón con la plaga púrpura / tengo el virus en los pensamientos / tengo el virus en la escritura / eu tenho fé que o vírus me fará inmortal / tengo el virus en el reloj de la cocina / sou um viado com a peste violeta / tengo el virus en los pies descalzos / tengo el virus en el vacío de mi habitación / guardo el sobre del diagnóstico / me hice la prueba 19 veces en 2 meses para comprobar que tengo el virus / o vírus escorre meu café / soy inmunodeficiente / soy unx humanx inmune a la muerte / el virus me hará inmortal / tengo el virus de Freddie / tengo los dientes y el virus de Freddie / tengo el virus en la piel negra y reseca / soy negro y maricón / soy negro, maricón y pobre / soy negro, maricón, pobre y anarquista / soy negro, maricón, pobre y anarquista / soy negro, maricón, pobre, anarquista y un dragón / soy negro, maricón, pobre, anarquista, un dragón y tengo el virus / sou preto, viado, pobre, bicha brava, um cara souzinho e eu tenho o vírus /

tengo el virus en el océano peligroso / PROFUNDO / OSCURO de mi sangre.

Queen of the Virus

ANDREA ALEJANDRO FREIRE F.,
TRANSLATED BY JESSICA LANAY

I have the virus / I have the inoculated virus / I have the virus inoculated under my tongue / I have the blistered tongue / I have the blistered tongue over my hand / I have the hand overflowing with the virus / I have sex filled with the virus / I have a life filled with the virus / I have the virus in my eyes / The virus runs from my nose / I have the virus in my hard hair / eu tenho o vírus em minhas palabras / I have the virus in the storm of my blood / faggot, I am a faggot with the pink plague / I am a faggot with the purple plague / I have the virus in my thoughts / I have the virus in my writing / eu tenho fé que o vírus me fará inmortal / I have the virus on the kitchen clock / sou um viado com a peste violeta / I have the virus in my bare feet / I have the virus in the emptiness of my room / I guard the envelope with the diagnosis / I did the test nineteen times in two months to prove I have the virus / o vírus escorre meu café / I am immunodeficient / I am unx humanx immune to death / the virus will make me immortal / I have Freddie's virus / I have Freddie's teeth and Freddie's virus / I have the virus in my dry Black skin / I am a Black faggot / I am a poor, Black faggot / I am a poor, anarchist Black faggot / I am a poor, anarchist, Black faggot and a dragon / I am a poor, anarchist Black faggot and a dragon and I have the virus / sou preto, viado, pobre, bicha brava, um cara souzinho e eu tenho o vírus /

I have the virus in the dangerous / DEEP / DARK / ocean / of my blood.

Translator's Note

JESSICA LANAY

THE REPLACEMENT of the feminine "-a" and the masculine "-o" at the end of gendered Spanish nouns, the articles "una" and "uno," and occasionally "el" and "la" with an "-x" is a political, spiritual, and social rejection by the nonbinary and LGBTQIA2+ communities of their erasure by the enforcement of the gendered construction found in Spanish from Latin America, the Caribbean, and Spain. The refusal to use the ungendered tense of "vos" is a rejection of the classist and racist implications behind the use of "vos" as a more acceptable/respectable/authentic Spanish that approximates the dialect spoken in Spain. The translator also wants to emphasize that the use of the ungendered "-x" is not replaceable with Latinate uses of the masculine "-tor" and the feminine "-trix." With these political, social, and spiritual contingencies in mind, the translator has maintained the uses of the ungendered "-x" and declined to translate them to preserve the very important and vital intent of the poet. There is only one place where the ungendered "-x" construction is not preserved: in the fourth line of "Lx DragOna." There the poet wrote, "Yo soy unx milagro de carne," which was translated to "I am a miracle of flesh" to preserve the affectual impact of the line.

The Portuguese lines found in "La reina del virus" were not translated, as they signal the complicated intersections of Blackness, Brazilian nationalism, Ecuadorian nationalism, and Indigeneity that play out in the Amazonian regions of South America.

In the poem "Electra" the phrase "yo tengo" can in many instances be translated, for example, from "Tengo la garganta atravesada por el silencio, aún" to "My throat is crossed by silence, still." But the translator preserves the "I have" verb construction in English to emphasize the state of possession, to maintain the repetition of the phrase in the original "Electra," and to gesture toward the tendency in global Black vernacular, including Black English, to use the phrase "I have."

Also in "Electra," the line "Mis venas huyeron de su caudal y el río se desbordó" was translated to "My veins fled their banks and the river overflowed" to maintain the extended metaphor and image over a direct translation.

In most if not all instances not explained above, the translator has preserved a direct translation as long as the poetics of the poet's intent are not interrupted.

[April 2020]

you (a short queer love story)

DES JACKSON

~~Your eyes are dark with stars and galaxies.~~
I promised you I would spare you the cliché love poetry, because you deserve more.

Your eyes always beg the question. What is it? Whimpering with your brows, softening with every blink and every brush of your lashes on my cheeks when you are sleeping next to me. Everything about you is like that, so dark and so curious, as if a whole universe lies dormant within you; as if whole lifetimes have lived in and through you. Querying. Like a shadow, like a mystery, like a secret I will forever keep—in the mist.

Their voice is passing notes in class when the teacher isn't looking. Slick and cool and tickling my skin. My fingers, trembling during the handoff. My hands, trembling when they hold them. Your skin is so soft and I don't know how. Your laugh takes me home, holds me, and carries me when I am too weak to walk.

To talk. To laugh. To cry. I am never too weak to feel your body on mine. I am never too weak to feel your life in mine.

Your mind, your thoughts, everything you (are). You are unreal. The divine love and mind you own are unfathomable in this world of mine.

We were smoking. That bong could never get the best of me, but it always got the best of you. We were in your grandparents' garage. My stomach hurt, hit with the iron fist, I could smell the alcohol on your tongue, I could feel the moths and bugs landing on my warm, moist skin—thirsty, but I was more. I was thirsty for your touch, your fingers, your confession of love. I was in a drought and the storms raging in your eyes promised sacred libations.

It was hot and humid, our usual summer temperament, and with every gentle breeze, a sigh from the trees, we inched closer, noses touching. I close my eyes and can still feel your breath dancing on my skin like a million ballerinas to a Mozart symphony, the melody you sang from your lips. Your hands on my back, reaching and scratching tree branches, in the wind to sweet dances,

my heart prances. You leaned in close and if I'd closed my eyes, I'd have known the second you pulled away. I am never too weak to feel your breath mingling with mine. You were never scared. I was nervous, more nervous than when I got called into the principal's office for the first time in kindergarten. I was on my toes, reaching for the stars you hide in your eyes. I made a wish and your lips pressed to mine before I could contest.

When I am around you, I feel a wholeness unlike any other. Like I'm safe. Like I'm here. Like I exist. My knees go weak, the typical response, and my heart feels like it's trying to break out of its cage and go home to yours. I feel warm. I feel warmth. I feel light. I feel enlightened.

When I am around you, I wouldn't imagine being anywhere else. Because anywhere else would be a world I only knew before you, lonely and cold. *I have an idea, let's grow old, together.* Along with all the stories my grandma told.

I pull these words from my gut and leave them to rot

LITTLE WREN

space. I couldn't hear the sounds of you screaming for help. your breath got lost in the vacuum. I keep my desires locked close, a smile and kind demeanor my suit against the world's bitter ways. would it be wrong to say I don't trust y'all to love me? would it be wrong to admit I don't trust your protection? I was born to labor. and everyone who meets me takes. anything else is temporary and leaves a bigger scar than it can soothe.

beware those who string silken words around you like a necklace. while you stroke the pearls, the words tighten to form a collar.

maybe I should trust more. but how could I? I was born and learned words were knives: quick and sharp and exact, cruel if handled incorrectly. I cannot be filleted and deboned again. I rebuilt myself with frills and stuffed cotton. my next self would only be the words I am writing to you now.

protect your heart. protect you.

Disonancia

PHOENIX RÍSZING

I went on a date
with a Dominican once.
They asked me what I was mixed with,
to which I replied,
Puerto Rican and Black.

Their face tightened
like an angry fist.
*Ew—don't tell people you're **Black**.*
Just say you're Puerto Rican.

What they didn't realize
was that they, too, were Black.
I just didn't love myself enough
to enlighten them.

Black Love

PHOENIX RÍSZING

In between my arms
two hearts beat
like they were made for each other.
How did I get so lucky?
To find love in a hopeless place?
In a broken state?
With her
all expectations are erased.
Her skin melts into my hands
like a Kit Kat bar left under the sun;
I watch it disappear
as it drips sweet love
down my sheets.
My Black queen.

Her smile is my doorway
to another dimension.
Life is suddenly heading
in a new direction.
A foreign place
but a happier one.
I don't know what the future holds
But I know
I want to see her there again.
Even if it's for a brief moment—
like those gentle kisses she gives me
so freely.
Or in the timeless place
we call *the now*.

Neither of us controlled
by psychological time.
No need to rewind to the past
when every new moment with her
feels better than the last.
Feels like
I'm moving too fast
for me to comprehend this
but love was never meant to be understood.
Love is only meant to be felt.

I've never experienced another soul
with this kind of intensity.
Does this mean
that she is meant for me?
With her
nothing and everything
makes sense.
With her,
all things are lost and found.
Even myself.

Lost in her affection
And found again in her presence.
Her voice turns my room
into another galaxy.
The depth of her soul
alters my reality.
Our connection
has shifted my perception of love
and now my heart is overflowing
with a beacon of light
where she ignites the fire.

How did I get so lucky?
To find someone
I wasn't even searching for?
If freedom was a place
it would be in her arms.

In the sound waves of her laugh.
In between her alien fingers and marshmallow lips.
It would be anywhere
and everywhere that she is
because touching her feels
like the sweetest place
I've never been.

She is the physical manifestation
of what I've always
asked the universe for.
But I'm afraid of love
because with love

always comes loss.

A Thank You Note

SASHA LAMPREA AREVALO

I woke up this morning and stretched my limbs.
Brown skin, a bit dry, not meant for the cold or these American winters.
I took off my bonnet to reveal hair that has not been slicked down,
pareces un sol I hear my mother's voice in my head.

What a beautiful comparison.

I look outside and I breathe in and I stand in my power.

To the women who walk steadily and from whose footsteps flowers sprout,
To the women whose skin is the color of the earth,
To the women whose hips sway and tell the wind which way to blow,
To the women whose hair grows and expands seeking the water in the air,
trying to soak up the essence of life,
To the women whose spirits continue to hold, guide, & comfort me,
To the women whose bodies embody fire and warmth,
To the women whose bones have crossed oceans, mountains, & deserts,
To the women simultaneously coveted and hated,
To the women who speak to me and ask for un cafecito con algo dulce to be
left at their altar,
To the women who invented the concept of resilience and never called it
anything other than living,
To the women whose names have been forgotten,
To the women who whisper in my ear not to discard pineapple peels, but to
boil them with rice, panela, cloves, and cinnamon sticks instead,
(Is this ancestral memory? The knowledge of recipes I don't remember
learning?)
To the women whose bodies never knew rest,
To the women who have made me,
To the women whose blood flows through my veins,

I thank you.

An Offering

SA SMYTHE

Stop me if you've heard this one before
So that I can tell it again, and savor it.
I am here, yet they think of me as a relic.
Not forgotten, but unglorified
A rough beast with a hashtagged accent of defeat,
A weak heart, and a Bethlehem slouch.

I often find myself both sought after and shunned—
Unable to speak my own name if I wanted—eternally emptied,
Made to mourn the loss of any meaning I might yet make
Like a silenced clap of thunder, technicolor turned to ashes.
It seems that so many I've loved have wanted me dead,
Ground down into the ancestral mosaic of past and present gods.

Earthly siblings, sweet apparitions: can we sanctify ourselves into
new life? I cannot warn the others of the coming storm alone,
Cannot take shelter from storms already here, and look! Just look.
Everywhere blood clings to the leaves, soot gnaws at the lungs
There's no water for miles, and soon all you can say is:
Well, we should've listened for the thunder.

Still, I was not the first to dream another world,
To crave the teeming darkness of the ocean floor,
Stories I would never fully know. With this I exalt myself,
Shapeshift into my harbinger skin. We have always been on the move.
Lithe and wild and dangerous, we grow new lungs,
Spread our palms across the dirt and tend to new leaves.

But I can never forget the body that came before.
Acidic grief dries out along the cracks in this new flesh,

Phantom bruises from when them did hush up the clap, thief the color.
I divine myself as Ochumaré, a messenger with an offering
That you may call me rainbow serpent,
Sibling, lover, or freedom traveler

That in case language doesn't express desire, but hides it,
You must remember to reach only for the neither thing,
To be righteously unashamed of this grief until the otherwise comes
Until that time when we may name ourselves whole, if not holy,
And stop eulogizing the project of living long enough to see
That it has yet to come, and so can never die.

FUTURES

Madrenuestra

YOLANDA ARROYO PIZARRO

Madre Nuestra que estás en la Infinitud
Santificades sean tus nombres, tus pronombres
las elles, las todes, las equis y @rrobas
venga a nosotres tu reinado antimachista;
y hágase tu voluntad feminista
así en la Tierra como en la Cuerpa y en la Calle
así en nuestra cama-cielo
Danos hoy la Siembra de cada día
el fruto de nuestra Tierra y Mar
el agua de nuestras cascadas
Y perdona nuestros errores
el veneno enlatado, el agua embotellada, el plástico
la monogamia desleal, el poliamor sin ética
la religión malintencionada
la opresión de clases
y demás horrores del capitalismo
así como nosotres también perdonamos
las cadenas autoimpuestas y la no solidaridad;
no nos dejes caer en la misoginia, la macharranería, la homofobia, el
racismo,
los crímenes de odio, la xenofobia, la supremacía blanca, el fanatismo,
los feminicidios
en fin, líbranos Madre Nuestra de obrar con maldad
Aménashé

Madrenuestra

YOLANDA ARROYO PIZARRO,
TRANSLATED BY LAWRENCE SCHIMEL

Our Mother who art in Infinity
Hallowed be thy names, thy pronouns,
the *elles*, the *todes*, the *X* and the *@*,
thy anti-sexist kingdom come unto us,
and thy feminist will be done
on Earth as it is in the Body and in the Street
as it is in our heaven-bed.
Give us this day our daily Seed
the fruit of our Earth and Sea,
the water of our cascades.
And forgive us our errors,
canned venom, bottled water, plastic,
disloyal monogamy, ethic-less polyamory,
ill-intentioned religion,
class oppression
and the other horrors of capitalism,
just as we forgive ourselves
our self-imposed chains and lack of solidarity;
let us not fall into misogyny, toxic masculinity, homophobia, racism,
hate crimes, xenophobia, white supremacy, fanaticism, femicides,
in short, deliver us, Our Mother, from operating with evil
Aménashé

existir

YOLANDA ARROYO PIZARRO

Tiene que existir un mundo en el que se pueda amar a más de una persona sin culpa. Que yo pueda besar ambas bocas sin sentir traición. Que una tríada de labios, a su vez, besen a otros labios con sosiego, sin conflicto. Que algune busque mis brazos, mis muslos, mis pechos solo cuando tengan sed de mí. Y que cuando haya hambre de otres, se logren abastecer con tales cuerpas. Tiene que existir un mundo en el que mi Amada sueñe con desear a otre sin contrición o pena. Que yo colabore en sus encuentros, que yo facilite sus romances sin envidia, sin maldad. Que la búsqueda de su felicidad no arda en celos; que la búsqueda de mi placer no sea motivo de guerra. Tiene que existir ese mundo. Deberá crearse, deberé crearlo. Debemos hacerlo todes nosotres.

exist

YOLANDA ARROYO PIZARRO,
TRANSLATED BY LAWRENCE SCHIMEL

A world must exist in which one can love more than one person without guilt. Where I can kiss both mouths without feeling betrayal. Where a triad of lips, in turn, kiss other lips with calm, without conflict. Where someone searches for my arms, my thighs, my breasts only when they thirst for me. And when the hunger is for others, those bodies are supplied. A world must exist in which my Beloved dreams of desiring another without contrition or shame. In which I contribute to their encounters, facilitating their romances with neither envy nor malice. Where the search for their happiness doesn't burn in jealousy; where the search for my pleasure is not a motive for war. That world must exist. It must be created, I must create it. We must make it all of us together.

Afrofeministamente

a mis Amoras las deseo afrofeministamente
lesboterroristamente
transgresoramente

les elijo Yo que soy el alfa
les hago juramentar un manifiesto
en el que prometen defender mi color de piel
de los intolerantes
de los racistas
de los blancoides
juran respetar mi antirracismo
y se disponen a derrocar las opresiones

a mis Amoras las erotizo afrofeministamente
apalabran el privilegio de cada una
lo colocan de espaldas a mí
de frente a mi bienestar
lo ofrendan en el portal de mi clítoris incoloro
cada noche

mis Amorxs afrorreparan en mi vientre
en mis brazos y en mi pecho
calman mi ansiedad si lloro por el mundo
destierran la supremacía blanca
derriban estatuas de Colón
y prenden en llamas iglesias
mis Amores no descienden del amo
su genealogía ha sido corroborada
llevan sus europeizantes apellidos
pero los repelen
reniegan su blanquitud

su mestizaje aclarado
su colorismo apocalíptico
viven avergonzadas de lo que sus ancestros hicieron con los míos

mis Amoras respetan mi linaje
se convierten en alfombra roja
sobre la cual camina
una reina negra kombilesa
estiro las manos
abro los dedos
embadurno en miel mis nudillos
y les doy de lamer

Afrofeministly

YOLANDA ARROYO PIZARRO,
TRANSLATED BY LAWRENCE SCHIMEL

I desire my Amoras afrofeministly
lesboterroristly
transgressively

I choose them, I who am the alpha
I make them swear a manifesto
in which they promise to defend the color of my skin
from the intolerant
from the racists
from the blancoids
they swear to respect my antiracism
and they get ready to abolish oppressions

I eroticize my Amoras afrofeministly
they discuss the privilege that each has
assume it with their backs to me
before my well-being
they offer it up on the portal of my colorless clitoris
every night

My Amoras afroheal in my belly
in my arms and on my breast
they calm my distress if I cry for the world
they evict white supremacy
knock down statues of Columbus
and light churches on fire
My Amoras don't descend from the master
their genealogy has been corroborated
they bear their Europeanizing surnames
but they repulse them

deny their whiteness
their lightening mestizaje
their apocalyptic colorism
they live ashamed of what their ancestors did with mine

my Amoras respect my lineage
they become a red carpet
above which strides
a black Kombilesa queen
I hold out my hands
I open my fingers
daub honey on my knuckles
and let them suckle

Decálogo de escritura afrofeminista radical

YOLANDA ARROYO PIZARRO

1. Contar una historia es irte en contra del mundo; escribe desde tu negritud subversiva. Sé afroversiva siempre.

2. Una historia finaliza con el lector; escribe desde los abusos que tu afrolesbofeminismo te ha costado.

3. Conviértete en Eleguá para tus personajes, abre sus caminos; escribe desde tu afrovisibilidad.

4. La voz narrativa o poética debe ser intensa y a la vez sosegada; escribe desde la vagina. Si no tienes, tómala prestada.

5. Haz uso del erotismo intencional; escribe desde un clítoris que se masturba. Si no tienes, tómalo prestado.

6. Resiste desde las palabras; escribe desde tu boca que besa a un clítoris que se masturba.

7. Lucha desde las palabras; escribe siempre desde la denuncia del machismo.

8. No escribas nunca a favor de los poderosos; escribe siempre desde la afrojusticia y la afroreparación.

9. Donde no puedas amar, no te detengas; escribe desde tu transgresor romance no monógamo.

10. Todos los decálogos que conozco, escritos antes que este, son de hombres cis; escribe en contra del Cis-tema patriarcal y desde la denuncia de todas las lgbttqfobias.

Decalogue of Radical Afrofeminist Writing

YOLANDA ARROYO PIZARRO,
TRANSLATED BY LAWRENCE SCHIMEL

1. To tell a story is to oppose the world; write from your subversive negritude. Always be afroversive.
2. A story ends with the reader; write from the abuses that your afrolesbofeminism have cost you.
3. Become Eleguá for your character, open their paths; write from your afrovisibility.
4. The narrative or poetic voice must be intense and at the same time calm; write from the vagina. If you lack one, borrow.
5. Make use of intentional eroticism; write from the clitoris that masturbates. If you lack one, borrow.
6. Resist from the word; write from your mouth that kisses a clitoris that masturbates.
7. Fight from the word; always write from a denouncement of machismo.
8. Never write in favor of the powerful; always write from afrojustice and afroreparation.
9. Where you can't love, don't dwell; write from your transgressive nonmonogamous romance.
10. All the decalogues I know, written before this one, are by cis men; write against the patriarchal cis-tem and from the denunciation of all lgbtqiaphobias.

Opening the Dominican Universe

ALEJANDRO HEREDIA

A CCORDING TO the Dominican Studies Institute at the City College of New York, in 1502 there lived a Black woman on the island of Ayiti who brought people into her hut and healed them. Letters between European officials dubbed her "the woman of the hospital."[1]

A few things strike my mind when I think of this story. First, it is striking that there was a Black person on the continent so early on in what we conceptualize as the colonial Americas. Second, the Black woman owned her hut and practiced medicine there, implying that she was a free woman. Lastly, a Black (potentially free) woman was influential enough that European officials wrote about her in high regard. To my mind, the story of the "woman of the hospital" is a prime example of the limitations and promises that live in the Dominican universe, the Dominican archive, and the Dominican imagination.

In *Colonial Phantoms*, Caribbean literature and history scholar Dixa Ramírez-D'Oleo writes:

> Ruling elites have been most able to record and disseminate their ideas of how to be in the world, but this is not the equivalent of subaltern subjects' appearing in official or elite records in ways that have little to do with their own agency. Subaltern subjects have often been recorded for posterity precisely at

---

1. "First Blacks in the Americas," Dominican Studies Institute, City College of New York, http://firstblacks.org/en/.

the moment of their punishment and subjugation in the pages of government documents as well as in "scientific," ethnographic, and travel accounts as imbricated with colonial and imperial projects. This is why those of us interested in understanding the lives of the non-elite, nonwhite subjects from earlier centuries have to sift through this deeply unjust archive, hoping we are reading "against the grain."[2]

Although the very few documents that mention the woman of the hospital depict her with high regard and not, as Ramírez-D'Oleo argues, at a moment of subjugation, the fact remains that the little we know about this woman has been written by the elite. We do not know her, or what her life might have been like in early colonial times, beyond what the colonial gaze might have imagined or deemed worthy of transcribing. The Dominican universe, at first sight, seems limited because of this very fact; the elites have written the story of that island for over five hundred years. There is so much we don't know.

As limiting as it might seem, for decades Dominicans in the diaspora have done significant work to expand the Dominican universe. Julia Álvarez, Junot Díaz, Josefina Baez, Angie Cruz, and Elizabeth Acevedo, to name the most celebrated writers: women and Black and poor and immigrant. These writers have expanded what it means to be Dominican beyond the white, upper-class, and male constructs that have dominated the way we, and others, view us as a people. Haitian writers like Edwidge Danticat and René Philoctète have also contributed greatly to the Dominican narrative by writing about the complex history of the island divided by two nations. As such, many writers from the island and in the diaspora work *against the grain* to unearth the stories that have not been told.[3]

The diaspora, however, is not without its own limitations. A lot of Dominican migrants and Dominican Americans become preoccupied with repeating the same narratives. The archetypical immigrant narrative is the first that comes to mind, which usually centers on the hardships of immigration, the language of harsh winters and longing for home. Much has also been written about the complexities of being Dominican American, at the

---

2. Dixa Ramírez-D'Oleo, *Colonial Phantoms: Belonging and Refusal in the Dominican Americas, from the 19th Century to the Present* (New York: NYU Press, 2018), 223.

3. For more on archives, reading, and writing, see Ann Laura Stoler, *Along the Archival Grain: Epistemic Anxieties and Colonial Common Sense* (Princeton, N.J.: Princeton University Press, 2009).

center of two cultures. Finally, our Dominican obsession, for which Dominicans have received the most literary acclaim: writing about the reign and aftermath of El Jefe's regime (here he remains nameless, only so that he will not drown another page).

I denote said tendency not as a critique but as an observation. Not to dictate what Dominican Americans should or shouldn't write about, or to argue against the fact that once, in its aftermath, narratives about the dictatorship were necessary. However, art demands that we tell a new thing or find a new way to tell it. Much has been written about the same thirty-one-year period. There is so much else of the Dominican universe to discover and expand upon.

Furthermore, while the narratives of immigration, Dominican American identity, and the dictatorship have permeated much of our literary production, there is a fourth narrative that has been imposed on us and has centered the way many folks in the United States understand Dominican people. On social media and otherwise, Dominicans have become the face of internalized anti-Blackness.

I once saw a meme that said: "On a scale from Dominican to Nigerian, how proud of your Blackness are you?" While I did laugh, as there is truth and humor in most stereotypes, I found the meme reductive. Not only of the complexities of Dominican history, which writers like Dixa Ramírez-D'Oleo and Ginetta Candelario have written about extensively, but also of the many people in the diaspora and on the island itself working tirelessly to dismantle anti-Blackness in our communities.

The issue of Dominican anti-Blackness is deeply historical and complicated. While we should continue to write about the deleterious effects of Dominican anti-Blackness on Dominicans, on Haitians, on all of us, it shouldn't be the only thing Dominicans are known for. At a public event a few years ago, I heard Silvio Torres-Saillant tackle the issue of Dominican anti-Blackness in the most succinct way I've ever heard someone speak on the topic. He said (and here I paraphrase), "It is not that Dominicans have historically denied their Blackness. It is, rather, that their Blackness has been denied to them." Knowledge of and connection to our African ancestry has been kept from us by the few men in power who have written our history to reflect themselves, not the larger population of the country. They (and now we) have erased Blackness from our newspapers, our hair salons, our museums, our leaders, and our institutions. The result is a people lost and confused about our own culture, lineage, and ancestry.

238 OPENING THE DOMINICAN UNIVERSE

It remains necessary here to state that while this is our brand of trauma, anti-Blackness plagues Black people everywhere in the Western Hemisphere, if not the world. To pathologize Dominicans as the most self-hating corner of the African diaspora is, again, reductive of violence done to us by those in power and negates the possibilities for an evolving Dominican imagination. We can hold Dominicans accountable for anti-Blackness, and at the same time leave space for the possibility of growth and renewal. We can do both.

If Blackness, so obviously central to who we are as a people, has been withheld from us, imagine what else we do not know as we should: our relationship to land; women's labor in every facet of society; and, especially important to me, the potential for queer possibilities.

Some of the work required is deeply historical and sociological. We need critical voices like Dixa Ramírez-D'Oleo, Ramona Hernández, Ginetta Candelario, and Carlos Ulises Decena to do the complex work of unearthing the history that has been withheld from us, and to create new frameworks through which to understand the complexities of who we are. Likewise, we need writers, prose writers and poets alike, to pick up the work where the analytical work cannot reach. To go to the places where only the imagination can go, and imagine the emotional, psychological, and spiritual lives of Dominicans whose stories have not been told yet.

For example, how might we open up the Dominican universe when we center a Black woman, a free person and a healer, as our origin story? What might we learn about ourselves then?

What if we write the woman of the hospital as a human being, not just as a disembodied symbol? Give her a name in Spanish, which she might have detested for all it stripped her of. Create a couple of patients she was particularly fond of. Imagine in great detail the hut she worked tirelessly to make her own. Draw up her mannerisms, the way she plaited her hair, the patience of her hands as she worked in the dry Caribbean heat. What if she fell in love with a man, he enslaved and she a free woman? Perhaps, driven by that timeless longing of separated lovers, she plotted with a few freedmen and they freed her beloved and everyone else, the first Black insurrection in the Americas. Maybe the two ran off, free, together. Out to the *monte*, the wild Dominican landscape. And maybe, just maybe, if we stretch her story through time, if we open up the Dominican universe, there she still is in the mountains, half a millennium later. Waiting for us to find her.

A Rewiring of the Senses

Considering Abolition

QUI DORIAN ALEXANDER

WHAT IF ABOLITION IS SOMETHING THAT GROWS?

What if abolition isn't a shattering thing, not a crashing thing, not a wrecking ball event? What if abolition is something that sprouts out of the wet places in our eyes, the broken places in our skin, the waiting places in our palms, the tremble holding in my mouth when I turn to you? What if abolition is something that grows?
—ALEXIS PAULINE GUMBS, *ABOLITION NOW!*

I HAVE TO defend my commitment to abolition so often that I sometimes forget why I am invested in the first place. The reason: To grow. To create the world anew. To generate the world we want to live in. Abolition to me is about liberation. Freedom. Our abilities to live lives that are self-determined, build communities that are interdependent and foster relationships with the land that respect the source we all come from. I believe abolition is a tool for us to grow our capacity for compassion. To stretch the limits of our hearts. To test what we mean when we say *we all deserve to be here.* To heal ourselves and each other. To come back in right relationship.[1] A way of seeing, knowing, and being alive in the world in more expansive ways than the ones we currently inhabit and accept.

What if we had more choices than right or wrong? What if we knew what we knew based on our shared love for information, rather than for

---

1. adrienne maree brown, *Emergent Strategy: Shaping Change, Changing Worlds* (Chico, Calif.: AK Press, 2017).

control of how people are to think? What if I got to be me and there was still plenty of space for you? What if we knew that there really was enough for all of us?

What would our world be like if we believed in abundance?

Abolition is more than the culmination of a struggle that bursts society open; abolition is the everyday actions we take to create spaces where we get to breathe together. *I look forward to the day when my body stops hurting from holding (on to) so much.*

Every day I get to make choices, some that do little to change my reality and others that blow holes in all that I thought I knew about how the world works. Every time we learn to care for each other through our trauma, through the anger in our bodies holding generations of misplaced grief, we move closer to god. *I met her, she's Black.*[2] When we commit to care, we move closer to our truth and find alignment with our purpose for being placed on this earth.

It is our duty to fight for our freedom,
It is our duty to win
We must love and support each other,
We have nothing to lose but our chains.

—ASSATA SHAKUR

Abolition gives me space to dream.

I'm tired of having to prove why my freedom is warranted. I am tired of swallowing my anger. I am tired of being tired. All school ever taught me was that if I was "good enough" I wouldn't feel so tired. Abolition teaches me that resting is an act of resistance. Rest helps me to dream about the world I want to live in and bring it to existence.

When I feel seen, connected, and joyful is when I am the most free.

I want to live in a world that teaches children that Blackness is as expansive as the universe. That gender is whatever one makes of it. That one is still deserving of love and care even after one makes mistakes. I want to live in a world that teaches children that our feelings are valuable guides with which to process our experiences. May we all live in a world that holds

---

2. While the origins of the phrase "I met god, she's Black" are hard to pin down, I use it here as a nod to Ntozake Shange's choreopoem *for colored girls who have considered suicide / when the rainbow is enuf*, in which she says, "I found God in myself, and I loved her fiercely."

space for the entirety of our emotions, without having to hide, deny, and "fix" them away. May we all live in a place that honors our wholeness.

I am a commitment to a durable and resilient heart.
—ALICIA GARZA

What does one do with the collective, intergenerational grief of being subject to dehumanization? Where do we teach that in textbooks? How does *that* feel in your body? Where do we teach about the emotional/spiritual inheritance of the Black diaspora? Where do we teach about what to do with that inheritance? What *do* we do with that? Abolition holds space for us to engage these questions. My heart breaks and swells, each time growing thicker with possibility.

We've always made magic.

Abolition clears the space for me to *remember*. To orient my life toward knowing myself outside of the bounds of being less than. To center the experience of being valued for who I am, not what I produce. To know that nothing about my being is a mistake. Abolition makes space to prioritize humanity and agency. It lets me be heart-forward, confronting the things that scare me the most. It is the practice of, commitment to, and reorientation toward confronting power that keeps me grounded in *why* I choose this work. I don't have to prove how much my heart (and bones) ache. In an abolitionist future, I just get to tend to them.

If you are silent about your pain, they'll kill you and say you enjoyed it.
—ZORA NEALE HURSTON

Every healing process has growing pains. Scar tissue.

I was so used to swallowing pain that my throat could no longer stand the burn. I had no choice but to address my healing. Every day I walked into a world that scolded me, policed me, and denied me a livable life. Every day I have to choose life, because every day something happens to remind me that the world doesn't care if Black trans people die. To commit to my own life, I had to make space for something I did not always understand: abolition.

Knowing who walks with you, then, becomes a spiritual injunctive to activate a conscious relationship with the spiritual energies with whom

one is accompanied, and who make it possible, in the words of Audre Lorde, "To do the work we came here to do."
                    —M. JACQUI ALEXANDER, *PEDAGOGIES OF CROSSING*

Little did I know abolition would clear the path for me to *do the work I came here to do.*[3] Abolition created the vision for me to live my everyday life with intention and attention to a purpose that was beyond the selling of my labor. It left space for me to remember that we were not always subject to a time of exploitation. There are ways to be with each other, support one another, and collectively develop a vision toward our freedom.

Challenging Immutable Truths: How We Learn Abolition

A Letter to My Kin:
Any/everything I ever learned about abolition did not come from a book. I learned through living in a body that is deemed disposable to the state, religious communities, and my own family. This Black, queer (trans) body. The body that houses my divine purpose is constantly under attack, under investigation, and under scrutiny. My body hypervisible and invisibilized in the same breath. So much of my life has been oriented around *being seen.* I am writing to tell you, you don't have to subscribe to demands of visibility, discipline, and punishment.

One of the first binaries we learn, right/wrong, creates the underbelly of punishment. We are taught that if we are wrong, we deserve to be punished. Every day, I was led to believe that I was *wrong.* Wrong for being Black, for having been born a "woman," for my queerness, for my trans reality, and wrong for wanting to talk about it. I internalized these lessons and believed I *deserved* to be punished, chastised, and surveilled.

I have never been incarcerated, but I've been criminalized my entire life. My mother told me that I could be different, that I could escape being one of them, one of the *bad people.* Living in a police state means being told that if we attend school, keep quiet, and blend in, everything will be okay. The idea of meritocracy leads us to believe that anyone can transcend their

---

3. Audre Lorde, *Sister Outsider* (Berkeley: Crossing Press, 1984).

oppressions and achieve the "American dream." That is not how power works. As a young person, I had done everything that was asked of me: not get pregnant, do drugs, or get locked up (as if that were a choice anyone could avoid under a system that criminalized racial, ethnic, gender, and sexual minorities). The promise of meritocracy and the American dream fell apart when I came out as trans. I was punished for choosing the truth; for choosing myself first. I disrupted the plan of meritocracy, which aims at producing governable communities that can be immediately punished if out of line. My body shifted and I became one of those *bad people*; an undesirable subject for choosing bodily sovereignty instead of submission. The first thing my mother asked me when I told her I was trans was, "*Who's going to love you?*" Hearing this question, I realized that my mother had internalized the state projects of gendered and racial discipline. In my mother's question, the assumption was that my body made me unlovable, untrustworthy, and unforgivable.

I'm writing to tell you that you don't deserve criminalization, surveillance, discipline, and submission.

How do I know? I've only begun to wrap my head around it in an effort to make meaning of my existence. My physical body is a manifestation of a blurred good/bad binary: What makes one a man or a woman, is it one's body? One's presentation? Is it how one thinks? How one acts? *Who knows?*

My body is a *rewiring of the senses*, a guide I have made for myself toward freedom and liberation.[4] The scars on my chest represent the physical, emotional, and spiritual loss that is inherently part of change. I am the embodiment of a contradicting ideology. This is a way of knowing. An embodied understanding that binaries aren't as real as we think they are. Binaries don't inherently have to be oppressive, but many have become so because binaries promise order and organization, tools used by nations to dictate who is deserving of community and protection and who is not.

I'm writing to tell you that you can be whoever/however you want to be.

"That demand for the rewiring of the senses is even more provocative when the cycle of action, reflection and practice cannot be automatically transposed to a curriculum whose learning requirements are sometimes neither straightforward nor self-evident."[5] You will not learn this praxis in books, and you certainly won't learn this in school. What I can teach you

---

4. M. Jacqui Alexander, *Pedagogies of Crossing: Meditations on Feminism, Sexual Politics, Memory and the Sacred* (Durham, N.C.: Duke University Press, 2006), 308.

5. Alexander, *Pedagogies of Crossing*, 308.

is how to feel. Feel with all of your might. I will not make bad feelings go away, but I will always support you making your way through them. I will support the choices you make that bring you closer to joy, even if others describe them as criminal. I will teach you that it is OK to show your pain in an effort to transform it. I will teach you what it takes *to be transformed in the service of the work*.[6]

Everything you know about what it means to be static can be shifted. Everything you thought was fixed *was never broken*. We do not want to shift the truth for fear of losing the power that truth gives us access to. Fear of not knowing who we *really* are behind those truths. *I once got a tattoo that said "impermanence." I wanted a permanent reminder.*

"All that you touch, you change. All that you change, changes you."[7]

Buckle up, this is only half of the ride.

I'm writing to tell you that things will change in your life. Things that you think have broken your heart wide open. I'm writing to tell you that those are the moments and spaces that you can address to identify who you are. You have the power to write yourself into existence.

Even if you end up reading this letter in a book, remember it was written as an intervention. As a meditation. As a portal for you to engage with me in whatever time and space you find yourself in.

> *Be creative. Ingenious. Pursue excellence. But remember scholarship isn't just about books. Scholarship is about how to create the tools that will free us from oppression.*
> —M. JACQUI ALEXANDER, *PEDAGOGIES OF CROSSING*

May you be able to *feel* the expansiveness of y/our humanity . . .

In Struggle,
Your Kin

---

6. This is a reference to Mary Hooks's "Mandate," delivered in 2016. "The mandate for Black people in this time, is to avenge the suffering of our ancestors, earn the respect of future generations, and to be willing to be transformed in service to the work."

7. Octavia Butler, *Parable of the Sower* (New York: Four Walls Eight Windows, 1993), 11.

All Legs Lead to Naomi Campbell

DARREL ALEJANDRO HOLNES
for Rosebud

We wear "crowntis," gender-
bending crown/tiaras tilted to the side
like we LGB royalTy,
like we long legs on a catwalk, smoking
up the haus with our
hot sex-kitten heels
with our stomp and strut
until the windows are foggy
and the bloggers are out
of breath and edges,
until we've snatched
and slayed the runway at Fashion Week
wearing everything
China is selling online
that Americans haven't
yet Columbused.

When I cross the streets
of Kreuzberg, and you
the streets of Hong Kong,
there are no breadcrumb trails.
These big city streets
are wider than any runway
but still we toe in style
to the Späti for beer
or to the rooftop for
cockatoos and secret teas
with grandmothers-in-law
and ghosts who only speak Cantonese.
But still we stiletto

or loafer or boat shoe
while running upstairs,
while hanging from ladders,
while climbing from the rooftop
to the skies.

There are so few of us
left standing these days after
the nightclub shooting at Pulse in Orlando,
after the lobotomies or
electroshock therapy,
after AIDS,
after passing for straight,
after passing for white and white and white—

Naomi Campbell
is a sunset over
the 7 train on our way
to get dumplings with
your new partner
while reading poems
about your ex or horses in Iceland,
both of whom took you for a ride.
Naomi Campbell is
a dark shadow in a dream
your cousins don't realize
will save your uncle. Naomi Campbell
is a fire hydrant you unleash after
Romeo burnt my city down.

In another era, we are
locked-up loonies.
In another era, we are
deities. Tonight, we are
throwing Blackberry phones,
dark-juiced and dangerous,
at whoever dares
stand in our way
or tell us how or who to love.

Strut your stuff with me, Black Diamond.
Come on, let's swallow the sun
and burn bright into the night
until our bellies are filled with
so much hubris
no man can ever put our kinship or kind asunder.
Filled with so much hubris,
we put god herself to shame.

Inheritance 1

JEYDELYN MARTINEZ

I need to tell the story of generational curses
Of why the women in my family carry such deep sadness
In the pits of their bellies, hasta el tuétano
But the world continues regardless of their approval or need to rest
In fact
It urges them to put on their brave face, como si nada
They retreat to their grind each and every day to the point of puro
exhaustion
To wake up, rinse, repeat
A cycle.

I need to tell the story of generational curses.
Why the men in my family have not passed the age of 55
If they're "lucky enough" to get that far in the first place
Because, you see, they die long before their time
Never an elder, accelerated ancestors
Que Dios los bendiga
It starts, but doesn't end with abuelo José
A seasonal worker in NYC
Papá never made it back to the shores of Yabucoa and I wonder if my
mother sat there hoping he'd return
She was only 2, but then 47 when she learned her brother, his only son,
Left this land similarly, his body on the cold concrete lifeless, this past
August
And what about all abuela's siblings' "accidental" deaths
Who is remembering and honoring them?

I need to tell the story of generational curses
Because if I don't, how can I continue to dream of breaking them?

How can I know a world that begs me to enter, not devoid of pain
But conscious of wounds that have scarred over and those that yet
need healing

Elders, Ancestors, Guides
Do not keep us from the truth
Because the bits and pieces,
Bits and pieces are haunting as I look into my abuela, my mami's face
And see, in their eyes, their eternal waiting
To be relieved as the keepers of our stories
Our curses, our verdades, pa' liberar
As I look at all the pictures of what should have been,
what could have been.

I want to tell the story of generational curses
To keep us moving forward. There is no such thing as liberation with-
out grief.
There is no use for half-truths.
Cuéntame, cuéntanxs.

Inheritance 3

JEYDELYN MARTINEZ

It's the way sofrito hits the pot and consumes your sensory world
It's the way you announced you were no longer relaxing your hair
It's the way you move that cuerpo, that ass, praise it!

It's the way they tried to box away your Blackness and you continue to
unravel it,
fully enamored

It's the way you love, fuck, bloom
It's the way you are unafraid to heal
It's the way you are leading a generation
It's the way you realized you were never half, you were always whole

It's the way you see a generation marvel, ameliorate the ugly, the beautiful of what they inherit.

It's the way you see a way through.
It's the way you see a way to.
It's simply the way you . . .

EVOLUTION

PHOENIX RÍSZING

Sometimes I cry
for that little girl in me
that I can't recognize anymore.
That Afro-Boricua girl
who wears strength
like she wears lip gloss.
But today,
I am in love.
I am in love
with the way the sun hits my melanin.
How I laugh through pain.
How I still find reasons to love
the people who have hurt me.
Today I am in love
with the silence of their absence,
my vulnerability,
their mistakes,
and now,
my evolution.

Ain't I Latina?

No, I don't speak spanish,
but Taíno blood still
pumps through my veins.

No, I don't speak spanish,
but I've got brown skin and curls
that spiral like the DNA of my African ancestors.

No, I don't speak spanish,
but the beat of the conga
is in perfect harmony with my heart.

No, I don't speak spanish,
but I can teach you
how to dance salsa,
bachata, and merengue.

No, I don't speak spanish,
but I make my own sofrito
and can cook a mean plate of arroz
con habichuelas.

No, I don't speak spanish
but my mother will still
hit us with a chancleta
whenever she needs to.

No, I don't speak spanish,
but I can roll my *rs*
and still pronounce
Yo soy boricua

with a certain level
of pride.

No, I don't speak spanish
but I didn't know
I needed it to feel the rhythm of our music
that ignites my internal fire.

I didn't know
I needed it in order to feel the brutal hands
of oppression that we,
as a people,
endure.

No, I don't speak spanish
and that's okay
because my Native ancestors didn't speak it either
before they were colonized.

Black girls deserve

ARIANA BROWN

love
money
& safety
a kitchen stocked with spices
full plate made by someone who loves us
freedom to live the lives we dream of living
in our sleep, in our most fragile states
the world up in flames
the day breaking
& the silence after
support
safety
family
grocery money & a trip to the store
produce, junk food, recipes to reproduce
heirlooms
a hand to hold
the truth told with compassion
quiet celebrations & loud ones too
kindness in the mirror
to be celebrated
to be remembered
grace
to make mistakes
to start over (on our own terms)
the last slice of apple pie
a light left on in the doorway
a working cell phone
a ride to work provided without complaint
to be respected
to be heard

to keep everything that is ours
fresh towels after a bath
a driver's license and someone to teach us
a car
to be hardheaded
to be tenderheaded
to never pay rent
to owe nothing
to own ourselves & our image
to know we are most powerful with each other
to be ungovernable
to be thought of & cared for
language that calls us correctly
the beat, bounce & holler
the news from our point of view
the sun on our skin
silk on our pillows
the names of our enemies turned to dust & their bodies too
freedom in this life & the ones that follow
elders, ancestors, cousins & aunties
children & niblings & friends who nurse our soft parts
to be soft
to be loved
to be safe
to be forgiven
to be in charge
to take a break
to take the year off
to retire
elegance & laziness
cute shoes, comfortable shoes
a world that loves us back
to have no end in sight
we will go on forever
& never let you forget it
someone to still be there
to watch each other grow
to lay our heads on your shoulders
to be moisturized & braided up

someone to do our hair
& do it right the first time
a safe place to sleep
stillness, peace
a love we don't have to wait for
confidence we don't have to explain
more than your thoughts & prayers
an end to relentless pain
a different world
one we've worked for & would still deserve
even if we hadn't
the end of sadness that lasts too long
our favorite songs on a playlist
water to dip our toes in
to live close to those who support us
to be loved
to be soft
to be safe
1,000 days without hearing of death
the end of wealth & states
to be healthy, to have healthcare
to know what was kept from us
the names of plants & their uses
what to bury, water, or light on fire
what the wind carries
what the soil knows
where the water's been
what our grandmothers can't speak of but know to be true
everything not mentioned we don't yet know we need
to live to live to live to live to live to live to live

we deserve to live.

There Will Be

ARIANA BROWN

There are supposed to be people who care what happens to you
and there will be.

There is supposed to be someone who loves you and tells you so
and there will be.

There is supposed to be someone who loves you and tells you so and
means it and proves it
and there will be.

There will be love, kisses on the cheek, a hand on your lower back, a
look in the eyes saying you are wanted. There will be ease. Soft breathing, and your favorite foods. A warm animal crawling into bed to sleep
with you. There will be your family, your sisters, the Black girls you love
with ferocity, there is them and you together, and safety. There is love.
There will be everything you've dreamed. Your own peace. A life you
made. With others who love you and tell you and mean it and prove
it. There will only be death if it is natural, if it is time. There will be no
running out of time or running away or running in circles. There will
be rest. A comfortable place to lay your head. There will be your body
and its glorious shape, the nape of your neck, a healthy head of hair
no one will want to change. There will be you looking in a mirror and
smiling. There will be peace. And grounding. There will be the sound
of Black people laughing and eating and carrying on. And you will join
them to laugh and eat and carry on and say ridiculous, beautiful things.
There will be your things, your stuff, that no one will take from you.
There is love, enough to go around. There is your history, no longer a
shadow, but a collective reason to protect this world where things will
be. Where freedom lives. There will be studying in groups and questions for how to move forward. There will be people taking care of each
other. There will be warm weather and fruit popsicles and your cousins

holding you tight. There will be life. In this world, I am telling you, I pledge to you, there will be life. There will be reasons to stay, to play, to give, to ask, to learn, to know, to grow, to dance, to try, to not have to fight. There will be someone's hand in yours. There will be.

We Win!

IVANOVA VERAS DE JESÚS

In the mountains
There are plants,
And fruits,
And cows,
And chickens,
And fresh air,
And us.

Now, we constantly seek change,
We don't run from it,
It moves us forward.

Back then, we wished to be free
We chanted, we fought.
Every hope, every drop of blood
And still we never imagined this.

They are not killing us anymore,
We sit together and heal,
We walk side by side,
Dream by dream.

Being alive
Is no longer radical,
Nor extreme,
It is inevitable.

The present is eternity
And Forever is queer,
Black, joyful, trans,
Safe, honest, authentic.

The present is open, raw,
Heart-felt,
Shame-free,
Accountability-driven.

The present is tender, bitter-sweet, respect, ocean-deep,
Adorable, relief,
Certainty, shapeless.

The present is unconditional love,
Family holding space,
Hands holding each other,
Vulnerability protecting change.

The present is community-based,
Equity-centered,
Fear-free,
And it is ours.

Hothouse, Or, The Taking Back of the Provision Grounds

IRENE VÁZQUEZ

I DON'T MEAN TO ALARM YOU BUT / WE ARE NOT ALONE IN OUR BODIES / I DON'T MEAN TO ERASE YOUR AGENCY BUT / WE ARE LESS BODIES THAN BOTANICAL GARDENS / LESS INDIVID-UALS THAN A COLLECTION OF HOLY SACRAMENTS / WHAT I MEAN IS / I RECENTLY FOUND OUT THERE ARE TRILLIONS OF MICROORGANISMS IN THE GUT ALONE / BACTERIA VIRUSES & FUNGI / MORE THAN THE NUMBER OF HUMAN CELLS IN THE ENTIRE BODY

I MEAN / I ALWAYS HAD A SNEAKING SUSPICION WE EXCEEDED THIS ANATOMY / SUSTAINED BY SOMETHING SIMPLER AND PERHAPS, CLOSER TO GOD / SOMETHING MORE ANCIENT THAT KNOWS NO NAME / SOMETHING PASSED DOWN MORE PRE-CIOUS THAN PROPERTY / SO FUCK OFF BIG PHARMA / THESE IS OURS / I GREW THEM OURSELVES OR RATHER / MADE OF THE BODY A HOTHOUSE / GAVE THEM A PLACE TO GO WHERE THEY LIVE COLLECTIVELY AND RENT FREE

WHEN I AM LONELY IN THIS PANDEMIC EXISTENCE WE HAVE BEGUN TO CALL A LIFE / I IMAGINE THEM ALL MISS FRIZZLED UP IN MY DIGESTIVE SYSTEM / ON A MAGIC SCHOOL BUS RIDE IN THE TWISTS & TURNS OF MY INTESTINE / I HOPE THEY LAUGH UP IN THERE AND IT MAKES ME GASSY / I HOPE THEY CACKLE LIKE MY BEST FRIEND ANANYA / I HOPE THEY RING OUT WHEN THEY'VE WON AN ARGUMENT LIKE SID / I HOPE THEY THROW GROOVY PARTIES UP IN MY GUT LIKE CAROLINE / IN OTHER WORDS / I HOPE THEY LIKE TO BOOGIE / ENGAGING

IN WHATEVA KIND OF UNICELLULAR MOTION FLOATS THEY LITTLE BACTERIAL BOAT!

AS I WRITE THIS POEM / IMAGINE THEM NOURISHED BY MY LATE AFTERNOON SNACK / OR, WHATEVER LEFTOVERS I EAT STANDING / IN MY KITCHEN

AND AS LONG AS I AM HERE / ANTHROPOMORPHIZING BACTERIA THAT ARE NOT AWARE I HAVE A CONSCIOUSNESS / LET ME JUST SAY / OUR MICROBIOME HAS DONE MORE FOR US THAN ANY PRESIDENT EVER HAS, WHICH IS TO SAY / KEPT US ALIVE ON PURPOSE / DARE I SAY THAT OUR BACTERIA KNOW THAT RACE IS A FICTION BUT THEY TOO HAVE SEEN SOME SHIT GO DOWN IN THE PROVISION GROUNDS / / THEY HAVE KNOWN POISONED WATERS THAT PRECEDED US / & THEY WILL BE BETTER PREPARED FOR WHATEVER FUTURE IS TO COME /

WHEN I AM AT MY LOWEST / I HEAR THEM CALLING TO US / *O OUR CHILDREN OF LOUISIANA SILT / DELTA BABIES, UNBOUGHT / AND UNBOSSED / WE WISH YOU MUD AND MUCK / FROM YOUR MOTHER WE WERE FORMED / NOT BORN BUT GUIDING YOU THROUGH YOUR JOURNEY BACK TO THE EARTH / TO THE MUD ONE DAY / WE WILL RETURN / BOTH BEYOND & BECAUSE OF YOU / BUT HERE, IN THE POEM WE CAN BE ANYTHING / SO WE SYNTHESIZED VITAMINS & GAVE YOU RHYTHM / BROKE DOWN SIMPLE CARBOHYDRATES & SENT YOU MOXIE / WE PUSHED & PULLED YOU TO THE BEAT OF OUR ANCESTORS TO GIVE YOU THIS / THE GOD BODY*

SO WHEN WE EAT NOW / WE EAT SACRAMENT / WHEN WE LIVE NOW / WE LIVE GARDEN / WHEN WE FUCK / & JUMP / & SLEEP SOUNDLY IN THE NIGHT / WE ARE BOUNTIFUL / WE ARE MULTIPLE / WE ARE HOME

[9 February 2020]

i am scared to touch the world

DES JACKSON

because what if it crumbles under my fingers? what if it burns? what if i learn it's all a dream? what if it swallows me whole and burps me out and i get lost and never found? what if it makes me realize that this me i pretend to be was never really me no matter how hard i tried to be? i am always living in-and-through a fear, something, deep and petrifying and tainting this world so that i hide away from it. if i blossom and bloom will i be picked or crushed, or take up too much space and water and root too deep just to keep myself grounded? if i blossom and bloom, am i allowed to grow up and outward and take up space in this world? i want to feel, i want to let move in me the energy, the emotion that needs space to breathe. i reach out into the world, shakily, yet surely and warmly love reveals itself in my life, with hearts and souls and company and laughs and smiles that hold me when it's cold and dark and empty and lightless. when it's not, there is light in this world that touches me too. there is warmth in this world that i deserve to feel in me too. i am scared to touch the world but i do anyway.

[8 October 2020]

the white owl

DES JACKSON

with tears in my eyes along an ever-winding road
to (no)where in the silky soft night
across my path danced
a white owl.
drifting and wafting
soundlessly
it felt the burn
of my headlights on its wings
and dove for cover in the gentle grasses beside.
and there it stayed as i went along my way
though i slowed to awe i did not stop
though i slowed to awe it stared at me
and said

> all endings are beginnings, all beginnings are ends,
> all the love and all the care is all you need to transcend
> this old way of being and be born anew—
> may i symbolize the death of the old you.

and i blinked the tears out of my eyes and said aloud
is what i saw true? god, was that you?
frozen in fear and frozen in feeling
that soft shadowy owl left me reeling.
but yet already as i write this poem here
i feel the skin shedding that's kept me safe for years.
its thickness is reminiscent
of the leather, taught and teaching
me how to behave
but i no longer need it
if it's me i'm trying to save

Castillo San Cristóbal

JEHOIADA ZECHARIAH CALVIN

"Can you guess
what this room is?"

The damp air sticks to my skin, the walls
are stained, the
light from the hallway seems to dim, my
breath quickens.

Shivering, I wonder if you can see my exhale but
of course it's too dark.
My bones tug in pain, the shift from hot
humidity to
cold wet triggers a memory.

"¿Saben?"

My spirit knows cells.
The feeling lives in my body, has done so
for many lifetimes.
It knew it in the ships, in the belly of the whale.
I knew it when
we ran away together, cuando seguimos a Júpiter
en el cielo
hasta que nos reunimos, pensando que era La Estrella
del Norte.

And in this life

                    running from mania to depression to dysphoria to
                              fear of hospitalization to
                    a subconscious memory of a past life spent alone

the possibility
of incarceration is as high as the tallest tree
I have ever prayed to.

In this life, my brother calls me
from his cell
and when I see him in his orange shirt,
I can't help
but break down before he can even greet me.
I tell him
nothing is wrong when he asks,
that I just
miss him, that it's been so long.

It is this longing I have the deepest memory of.
Las vibraciones
han grabado estos secretos
en mis vértebras.
Cuando me duele, me acuerdo.

In the next life,
there are no cells to hold my brother, no cells to hold me,
no more longing, no more emptiness, just the sound
of a last exhale giving way to a cry of birth.

Prophecy

JEHOIADA ZECHARIAH CALVIN

I. BEFORE
I speak with the rhythm of the waves
to open up the portal,
to let the lake guide us
to our dreams of revolution,
to a world to come,
to the deaths we face
but always to be born again.

This is to say, grieve
when you need,
but always remember to wake up and watch
the sun dance on the lake.

II. HERE
With my siblings in my hands,
I dance left to right,
root in breast,
into liberation,
cantando las canciones que nos dejaron nuestres ancestres
para recordarnos que elles siempre supieron lo que es la libertad,
that this was just some time we had to fight through,
that the Creator
always had a plan,
and if we would just be still
and listen to the wind,
look to the flicker of the candle,
read the reflection in the mirror,
we would know.

III. BEGINNING AGAIN

They made up disorders they said made us run.
Called us crazy when we heard our ancestors.
But one day we rose up and finally
saw ourselves,
and the archive
in our bodies
reminded us
that we always
knew how
to be free.

Tomorrow,
as ancestors,
we blow the smoke of the incense
to catch your attention
and let you know
que siempre estaremos aquí
que nunca nos iremos
porque vivimos a través de ti,
juntes contigo,
para toda la eternidad.

When Dreaming of a Future Means Letting Go

ALAN PELAEZ LOPEZ

In the future
       there are no more nations
       no countries   no conquered land
       there is only *us*
       and when there are no more corporations
       or governments or nation-states to blame
       we'll have to learn to be accountable
       to one another and
       face some of the worst parts
       of who we once were

One day
       we will address the violent myth of mestizaje
       the romanticization of conquest
       and the logic that made many believe that Europe made *us*
       better
       and it'll finally be easy to be Black in Latin America
       those of us who are Indigenous will speak our languages
       and no longer be punished for it
       Asian Latinxs will no longer be asked for "papers"
       stereotypes about "Chinos" will be eradicated
       all Caribbean peoples will be able to travel freely
       and all sick, fat, and disabled people will live lives full of care
       & tenderness

In the future
       centuries will pass without a single queer and trans hate crime
       the world will forget they existed   a sign that we finally
                    learned to honor life

In the future
> we will look at ourselves in a mirror
> and say "fuck, I wasn't always a good relative"
> and it'll be hard, and it will never get any easier
> because building a world outside of violence requires daily
> commitment and work

I am inviting you to dream with me

I am asking you to believe
> in the reality that there is so much more to live for than
> nationalism
> so much more to strive for and families to build outside of
> cis-heterosexuality
> so much care available that we finally stop feeling shame for
> asking to be loved

I am asking you to believe
> in the reality that we have never needed nations to be human
> that we have never needed papers to be human
> that we have never needed governments to be human
> that we have never needed to speak the same language to be
> human

In the future
> there is no more abstract "latinidad"
> because that requires us to hold on to all the stories we tell
> about one another
> and not many include Black, Indigenous, Asian, sick, fat, dis-
> abled, or queer and trans kin

In the future, there is no abstract "latinidad"
> there is accountability
> daily practices of abolition
> courageous conversations that are valued
> and radical epistemological changes
> because that creates power and community care

I want all of us to be alive in the future

but are you ready for all we must do to get there?

What will you commit to?
>Will you give up all your fantasies of unity?
>>Will you give up your power? Your wealth? Your status?

Who will you be and how will you show up when all that's left is each other and the actions we took that we never dared be accountable to?

an invitation to play, a choreographer's offering

EHQS / IZAR

If you want: identify, play, and dance to your favorite song.
Allow your pelvis to lead your movement.
When the song is over, close your eyes and start shaking in place.
Shake off the things that are no longer serving you for as long as you
need.

If you're tired, lean into it and rest by making your way to the floor.
Once you're there, notice the edges of your body.
What parts of you are making contact with the floor?
Are you comfortable?
Can you shift slightly to make yourself even more comfortable?
Move perpetually toward comfort.
Play with this for a while.

Next, notice the texture of your clothes against your skin and the
texture of those clothes against the floor. Notice the temperature of
your body, the temperature of the floor, the temperature of your room.
Notice the space your body occupies in the space that you are in.
Spaces within spaces within spaces.

Are there plants in your space?
If so, notice them.
Call out their names.
Thank them.

If you're up for it, allow yourself to tune in to the fluids of your body.
We are mostly water, but there is also the blood, urine, cerebrospinal
fluid, cum, tears. Focus on just one of these, the one that calls to you

right now, and move from this place. Or don't move, and meditate on this fluid running through and being created through your body. Spend some time here.

When you're ready, take a break, write down some reflections, and if you're up for it, take a walk for as long as you need in your neighborhood.

As you're walking, allow each step to deepen your relationship to the Earth, whatever and however that shows up for you.

Give yourself permission to wander, to be encountered, and to encounter yourself in unexpected ways.

Take yourself out to dinner and from there invite synchronicity to lead you through the rest of your evening . . .

The choices you make are and always have been yours to make.

Let me know how it goes.

Coda

ALAN PELAEZ LOPEZ

Escribo pensando en una venganza. En la traición que colectivamente estamos materializando a esta cultura construida desde la razón hétero-blanca porque a lxs hijxs de las mujeres negras muy pocas veces nos trataron con amor.
(I write thinking of revenge. In the betrayal that we are collectively materializing against this culture built from white hetero reason because we, the children of black women, were rarely treated with love.)
—JOHAN MIJAIL, 2018

White supremacy . . . tries to kill the imagination. . . . Part of my survival was being able to imagine myself into the future.
—LADY DANE FIGUEROA EDIDI, 2022

IN DECEMBER of 2022, I organized a panel conversation titled "Transing Afro-Latinx Studies and Identity" at New York University, in which Nigerian, Cuban, Indigenous trans* writer Lady Dane Figueroa Edidi explained that her "survival" depended on "being able to imagine [herself] into the future." Her words stuck with me for months but I did not know why. Perhaps I had never thought about myself in the future. Before I turned thirty, I published a poem titled "On the occasion that i die before i'm thirty" in the independent digital magazine *Catapult.* That specific poem was written at a time in my life when I felt like I was more acquainted with death than life. Over a Zoom panel conversation, Figueroa Edidi's words turned all the air molecules around me into a spiritually charged form of oxygen that refilled my lungs and helped me recommit to living. That night, I took out Johan Mijail's *Manifiesto Antirracista: Escrituras para una biografía inmigrante,* which was the first Spanish-language book I had read written by a Black, trans*, Caribbean migrant, and I wept with joy. As someone who grew up an "illegal alien" in the United States, books were the only places where I could escape my reality as a legally undocumented Black Zapotec trans* person. On the night of the NYU panel, I lay in bed thinking about Lady Dane Figueroa Edidi and Johan Mijail's notion of "venganza" against "la razón hétero-blanca," and I whispered to myself, "I hope that this edited volume is something that makes Mijail proud," meaning, I hope that this volume enacts revenge against the same hetero- and white-supremacist logic that continuously attempts to stop queer and trans* Black freedom.[1]

When Language Broke Open is not just an edited volume; it is an object, an archive, and a document that speaks to different geographic, temporal, and ideological understandings of Black aliveness by people who are queer and/or trans* of Latin American descent.[2] Documentation is something not all of us have had. Some of us were born in countries where archives of Black Latin American, Afro-Latinx, and/or Afro-Caribbean families, resistance movements, and newspapers were seen as threats and burned, erased, or hidden. Others grew up in geographies where we were told our kind didn't have a history, a story, or a place in the community. And some of us quite literally grew up undocumented: without legal permission to reside in the United States or in the Latin American and Caribbean countries our families saw themselves forced to migrate to. Therefore, this collection does the work of counterdocumenting not only ourselves as queer and trans* Black writers of Latin American descent, but those who came before us: the ones our grandparents never mention because of shame or to protect their right to opacity, or those who are always mentioned but whose stories are curated to leave out the queer, the trans*, the agender, the hypersexual, the nonsexual, and our darker-skinned relatives, because, after all, colorism thrives in Black communities.

Memory may not be something we all have access to, but memory is something we have made, insisted on, mourned over, and committed to through these pages. No one can tell us that we ain't got no canon. We are not the first, we're just the first to have been able to access each other primarily through social media, WhatsApp messages, and friends of a friend

1. Johan Mijail, *Manifiesto Antirracista: Escrituras para una biografía inmigrante* (Santiago: Los Libros de la Mujer Rota, 2018).
2. Here, I use "Black aliveness" in reference to the work of Black cultural and literary studies scholar Kevin E. Quashie, who argues that "to behold such aliveness, we have to imagine a black world . . . we have to imagine a black world so as to surpass the everywhere and everyway of black death, of blackness that is understood only through such vocabulary." For more, see Kevin Everod Quashie, *Black Aliveness, or a Poetics of Being* (Durham, N.C.: Duke University Press, 2021).

of a friend. Much like the work of *This Bridge Called My Back: Writings by Radical Women of Color* (1981) and *Our Caribbean: A Gathering of Lesbian and Gay Writing from the Antilles* (2008), *When Language Broke Open* honors and celebrates first and foremost the fact that we are alive, writing, and speaking even when the language doesn't feel complete, and thus it spills and splashes. I'm not afraid of the spill because, if it isn't obvious, we're willing to clean up, not the fuckery of others, but the fuckery we are identifying and addressing in our own personal lives.

As I put closure to this artifact, the writing of Afro-Venezuelan trans* artist Iki Yos Piña Narváez Flores rings in my head: "Ningún cuerpx negrx queer sin amor sobrevive la *social death*" (No black queer body without love survives social death).[3] Death is all around us, it is difficult not to think about it, and because of this we need care. *When Language Broke Open* engages care as a methodology precisely because Black aliveness is our terminus. As Puerto Rican trans* writer Sora Ferri writes in these pages, "quiero llegar al punto de mis tías / and look at death as a portal / to a new relationship." But to do that we need to live in a world that celebrates us, so that death is not something we anticipate due to our race, gender, sexuality, or heritage, but something which comes as an organic process of life. I, like Ferri, want to "look at death as a portal / to a new relationship" because, as Mexican American writer des jackson writes, "i am scared to touch the world but i do anyway." For us to live in a future where death is a portal to rest and renewal, non-Black people need to prioritize trans* and dark-skinned Black lives. This also means that within our own Black community, we need to betray any approximations some of us may have to whiteness and ideologies of whiteness, cis-heterosexual ideologies, gender binaries, and limited understandings of Black queer and trans* futures.

The work that has been proposed by writers like Qui Dorian Alexander, Alejandro Heredia, Ariana Brown, Yolanda Arroyo Pizarro, and Breena Nuñez, for example, encourages our diasporic kin to approach narrativity as a political action that activates what Heredia names a new "universe." These universes require rigorous questions like the ones posed by Dorian Alexander: "What if I got to be me and there was still plenty of space for you? What if we knew that there really was enough for all of us?" When these questions are attended to, we can finally begin to operate not from

---

3. Iki Yos Piña Narváez Flores, "Las aves del paraíso," in *La fragilidad del cuerpo amado: Escritos cuir y trans en torno a la politicidad del dolor* (Madrid: Editorial Contina Me Tienes, 2019).

a place of scarcity, but a place of abundance. I am unsure of how many times I can reiterate this sentiment, but I do not believe that this is the first collection of queer and trans* Black writers of Latin American descent. I want to insist that queer and trans* Black writers of Latin American descent gathered, wrote, published each other, and self-published in their own private communities. Insisting on this speculative past negates the trope that we have not spoken, written, and/or imagined together. We have gathered, written, and imagined, and we will continue to do so. From this day forward, my hope for all of us is that we take Yolanda Arroyo Pizarro's "Decálogo de escritura afrofeminista radical" (Decalogue of Radical Afrofeminist Writing) as a serious guide (/method) of relationality that names and deconstructs the coloniality of race, gender, and sexuality, and that in doing so, we arrive at the doorstep of the future.

In the future, we live. In the future, we live gloriously.

CONTRIBUTORS

Alan Pelaez Lopez (b. 1993, Mexico) is an interdisciplinary writer, visual artist, and theorist from Oaxaca, México. In their poetic and visual work, Alan attends to questions of Black futures, trans* kinship, and Zapotec (un)belonging. Their theoretical writing excavates and addresses the intimate relationship between settler colonialism, forced migration, and the global circuit of anti-Black violence. They are the author of *Intergalactic Travels: poems from a fugitive alien* (The Operating System, 2020), which was a finalist for the International Latino Book Award, and *to love and mourn in the age of displacement* (Nomadic Press, 2020). In 2022, Pelaez Lopez was awarded a Ruth Lilly and Dorothy Sargent Rosenberg Poetry Fellowship from the Poetry Foundation, and a Miriam Jiménez Román Fellowship from New York University's The Latinx Project. Alan's writing can be found in *Women's Studies Quarterly*, *Teen Vogue*, *Refinery29*, *Best American Experimental Writing*, and other places. Pelaez Lopez earned a PhD from the University of California, Berkeley, was an assistant professor of queer and trans* ethnic studies housed in the Department of Race and Resistance Studies at San Francisco State University, and is currently an assistant professor in the Department of Chicanx/e Studies at the University of California, Davis, where they teach classes on Chicanx, Afro-Latinx, and Caribbean literature and visual culture.

Zoë Gamell Brown (b. 1992, United States) is a Guyanese American integrative artist, educator, and storyteller based in Kalapuya Ilihi. Her work explores Boviander ecologies extending from the Caribbean to the Gulf through ancestral practices invoked by ceramic sculptures, culinary catharsis, creative nonfiction, experimental video, photopoetry, restorative cartography, and sonic arts. Brown is a doctoral student in the University of Oregon's Indigenous, Race, and Ethnic Studies Department, where they are a member of the inaugural cohort. In 2020, she founded Fernland Studios to reimagine environmentalism through artist residencies, educational retreats, and writing workshops for and with communities of color in the Pacific Northwest. Brown was a Digital Evolution/Artist Retention Fellow through the Caribbean Cultural Center African Diaspora Institute and a Louise Westling Distinguished Environmental Justice Fellowship through the Pacific Northwest Racial and Climate Justice Futures Institute.

Tirzah Sheppard (b. 1997, United States) has been writing poems since they were a young child. Always a passionate writer and storyteller, Tirzah now explores visual mediums like film and photography. Their current project, *The Black Love Archive*, shows queer Black modern love through in-depth interviews and photography. As a Black lesbian of Caribbean, Black Southern, and Panamanian heritage, she aims to share diverse, intersectional stories through her artwork. In her free time she enjoys spending time with loved ones, studying Brazilian Portuguese, dancing, and daydreaming of a world where Black people are free.

Armando Alleyne (b. 1959, United States) is an artist and a poet. He grew up in Lower Manhattan and graduated from the City College of New York with a BA in education and fine arts in 1983. Alleyne's painted and collaged renditions of jazz musicians, Afro-Latin singers, boxers, and also family members and friends have a rhythm all their own. Parallel to his practice of painting portraits of Black icons, he allows elements of his lived experience to take form in his work. Never shying away from the seminal, the sensual, or the political, Alleyne's lifetime of paintings tell a story of how we are subject to our city and how in it we can search for the tools to heal. In 2021, Alleyne's first monograph, *A Few of My Favorites*, was published by Edition Patrick Frey. Alleyne lives and works in Brooklyn, New York.

Felene M. Cayetano (b. 1978, Belize) is a Belizean Garifuna librarian, author, mother, photographer, screenwriter, and director. She has published two collections of poetry and an anthology of short fiction by Belizean authors. She became a librarian in 2007, is a founding member of the Belizean Writers Guild, and serves on multiple boards of directors. Her portrait and nature photographs have been exhibited in Belize and are now available as NFTs. She wrote, directed, and edited her first narrative short film, *Sides*, in 2022. It features a lesbian couple in Belize with one closeted partner.

Janice Heather Hector (b. 1982, Saint Lucia) is from the simply beautiful Caribbean paradise Island of Saint Lucia, born into a seven-member family. Religion was the foundation of her upbringing, and so she turned to the world of poetry when she felt the need to express herself without judgment. She writes, "Poetry saved me. It became my great escape, my world away from the one I lived in, it became my sanctuary. My biggest goal is to one day achieve the accolade of Nobel Laureate for Poetry, one already held by my Saint Lucian poetry idol Sir Derek Walcott." Currently, Janice Heather Hector is a full-time civil servant, part-time student, and full-time poet, while tirelessly working on publishing a collection of her own. The long-term goal is to pursue a career where poetry is at the helm. "You may face many defeats in your life, but never let yourself be defeated." —Dr. Maya Angelou.

Clara Olivo (b. 1986, Turtle Island) is an Afro-Salvi poet living in diaspora. Born and raised in South Central L.A. to Salvadoran refugees, Clara weaves history and lived experience, creating diasporic poetry that amplifies ancestral power and pride. Writing for her lost inner child, Clara steps into her poetry with the intention of healing the hurts of her past and inspiring hope for the future. She's steadily building her reputation as a poet and spoken-word artist through the support and empowerment of the Alegría Writers Collective. Since finding her voice, she has performed in open mics and ceremonies from Seattle to Washington, D.C., and has been featured in publications such as *The South Seattle Emerald*, *Valiant Scribe*, and Quiet Lightning's Literary Mixtape. Clara lives in a quiet home on unceded Duwamish land with her partner, her dog, and an ever-growing number of houseplants.

Dr. Dora Santana (Brazil) is a Black Brazilian trans woman artist and scholar. She is an assistant professor in the Department of Gender and Women's Studies at the University of California, Berkeley. Her work has been published in the "Issue of Blackness" issue of *Transgender Studies Quarterly* (*TSQ*), under the title "Transitionings and Returnings: Experiments with the Poetics of Transatlantic Water," and *TSQ*'s issue "Trans in Las Americas," under the title "Mais Viva! Reassembling Transness, Blackness and Feminism."

Jehoiada Zechariah Calvin (b. 1997, United States) is a writer and a memory and zine maker from Chicago with family from the city by way of the South, and from Mexico City. He has been writing poetry for as long as he can remember and making zines since high school, and he put on his first performance art piece, *Liminal.*, in 2019. Jehoiada has self-published more than five zines and one chapbook, *Liminal. and Other Poems* (2020). Jehoiada's work has been published in magazines and other zines, including *Blue-Book Magazine* and *Sonku Magazine.* Jehoiada graduated from Amherst College in 2020 as a Black studies and Latinx and Latin American studies double major. Jehoiada currently works in cultural heritage while focusing on Black historical collections. Jehoiada's inspirations include his ancestors, Nina Simone, and Lake Michigan. Visit jehozcalvin.myportfoilio.com for more work by Jehoiada or to contact him.

Estrellx Halcyon Quetzal Supernova (EHQS) / IZAR (b. 1992, United States) admits that they are finally ready to move on. They frame choreography as embodied excavation, as an intimate practice that opens up portals toward giving oneself radical permission to dissent, celebrate, grieve, and rest. Estrellx envisions their performative and curatorial works as nomadic club spaces where generative dissonance, pleasure, and alternative subjectivities of the erotic emerge and give way to effervescent ecosystems. They are often creating choreographic scores where alchemical transmutation unfold through ritualistic activations. They implement qi energetics, club dancing, psychosomatic improvisation, and divination, among other tools, in their performative and curatorial languages. Their performative encuentrxs awaken templates for repatterning conditioning and inherited trauma, engendering remixed systems, alternative pathways, unexpected collaborations, and a dilated sense of time. Estrellx asks, "Are we celebrating or mourning or both? How do we work with what we have to redesign how we do everything? What do you really want and how exactly do you want it?" You can find out more about Estrellx and their macrovision, called The Universe of Rhizomatic Tenderness, on IG (corporealidades.sutiles, estrellx_supernova, stonehengepapi_soggycereal) and at www.estrellx-supernova.com.

Qui Dorian Alexander (b. 1986, United States) is a queer, trans, Black Puerto Rican scholar, educator, and organizer currently based in Tkaronto. They are an assistant professor of gender, sexuality, and trans studies in curriculum and pedagogy at OISE, University of Toronto. Their work and scholarship centers queer Black feminist praxis, Black trans studies, transformative justice, abolition, and healing justice. Their current research focus is on pedagogies of abolitionist praxis in the lived experience of Black trans folks. Grounded in their experiences as a community organizer, Qui views their scholarship as a place to articulate the cultural work they do in relation to their communities. Believing education is a practice of freedom, Qui strives to center personal transformation and healing in every educational space they have the honor to hold and co-create.

Sasha Lamprea Arevalo (b. 1991, Colombia) is a queer, Black, Latina, immigrant, Texas-based woman and mother continually seeking rest, joy, and a peaceful, authentic existence. Ni de aquí, ni de allá; she is from both and everywhere else her people have called home.

Yolanda Arroyo Pizarro (b. 1970, Puerto Rico) is a queer AfroPuerto-Rican writer who writes fiction, poetry, essays, and children's books. All of their writing (including these poems) challenges whiteness, heterocentrism, binary gender and gendered language, American colonialism, and more recently monogamy as well. Her short story collection *Las negras*, winner of the 2013 National Short Story Prize from the PEN Club of Puerto Rico, explores the limits of the development of female characters who challenge hierarchies of power. Her books *Caparazones*, *Lesbofilias*, and *Violeta* explore transgression from an openly visible lesbianism, whereas *Transcaribeñx* tackles and dismantles gender categories and identities from a Caribbean perspective.

Jeydelyn Martinez (b. 1994, United States) (she/her/ella) is a queer Afro-Boricua writer raised in the Midwest, with familial roots in Yabucoa. Jeydelyn composes poems, short stories, essays, and blog posts. Jeydelyn's writing aspires to unearth and traverse familial stories and wounds, womanhood, relationships, identity, and travel. "Inheritance 1" and "Inheritance 3" are Jeydelyn's first published poems.

Sora Ferri (b. 1994, Puerto Rico) identifies as a Black trans woman born in San Juan, Puerto Rico, to a Colombian mother and Puerto Rican father.

She has been loved into being by multiple communities tanto de Puerto Rico como de Seattle, Washington, and by her trans ancestors. She loves to write and currently works with other trans, cuir, and negrx creatives in documenting our lives in Puerto Rico on our terms. To see more of Sora's and her community's work, visit www.espicynipples.com.

Reva Santo (b. 1994, United States) is a storyteller and creative alchemist. She graduated in film studies from Columbia University, where she was awarded the Louis Sudler Prize in the Arts for her script "Ash(é)," and the Henry Evans Travel Fellowship to conduct arts-based research in the Caribbean. She has shown short films at Studio 1.0.6. Gallery, Miami Art Basel, PRIZM Art Fair, Pan African Film Festival, and more. Her written works have been published by *TOAN Mag*, Syla.Studio, and The Diaz Collections, among others. A researcher and avid learner, Reva is guided by her insatiable curiosity. Her creative practices and intellectual pursuits are languages for inquiry and tools for personal and collective healing. She creates transformative, alchemic works that heal and imagine new possibilities for the world. Her creative practice is predicated on an understanding that she is a continuation of her ancestors' greatest struggles, desires, and dreams.

Jessica Lanay (b. 1987, United States) is a Black feminist interdisciplinary writer, poet, and art journalist raised in Key West, Florida. Their/Her debut hybrid poetry collection, *am•phib•ian*, won the 2020 Naomi Long Madgett Poetry Prize judged by Toi Derricotte from Broadside Lotus Press. They/She is a Cave Canem and Callaloo Fellow. Their/Her poetry can be found in *Indiana Review*, *Prairie Schooner*, *Poet Lore*, and other publications. They/She has performed her poetry at the Brooklyn Museum, the Cave Canem and Bowery Presents First Book series, and with Brooklyn Poets. Their/Her personal and craft essays can be found in *Salt Hill Journal* and *Black Warrior Review*. Lanay's art writing can currently be found in *BOMB Magazine*, where she has interviewed artists such as El Anatsui, Howardena Pindell, Vanessa German, and Shikeith, among others. Their/Her art criticism can also be found in catalog contributions for the Andy Warhol Museum's exhibition *Fantasy America*, and the Washington Project for the Arts exhibition curated by Tsedaye Makonnen, *Black Women as/and the Living Archive*.

Malika Aisha (b. 1993, United States) is a queer AfroLatinx poet, born and raised in Bushwick, Brooklyn, with a BA in English language and literature from Ithaca College.

Ariana Brown (b. 1993, United States) is a queer Black Mexican American poet from the Southside of San Antonio, Texas, now based in Houston, Texas. She is the author of the poetry collections *We Are Owed.* (Grieveland, 2021) and *Sana Sana* (Game Over Books, 2020). Ariana's work investigates queer Black personhood in Mexican American spaces, Black relationality and girlhood, loneliness, and care. She holds a BA in African diaspora studies and Mexican American studies from UT Austin, an MFA in poetry from the University of Pittsburgh, and an MLS in library and information science from the University of North Texas. Ariana is a 2014 national collegiate poetry-slam champion and owes much of her practice to Black performance communities led by Black women poets from the South. She has been writing, performing, and teaching poetry for over ten years. Follow Ariana on Twitter and Instagram @ArianaThePoet.

Little Wren (b. 1999, United States) is a writer from Alabama with roots from St. Croix, the Dominican Republic, and Liberia. They write poetry and speculative fiction in long form. Their work questions the themes of home and belonging and our perceptions of reality through the lens of caste, gender, and geography. In imagining new and different worlds, Little Wren hopes to expand how we view care and community.

Raquelle Mayoral (b. 1987, United States) was born in Chicago into families with partial origins in the places now called the U.S. South and Ponce, Puerto Rico. They received their BA from Howard University in 2009 and their MFA from Antioch University–Los Angeles in 2016. They have taught creative writing workshops focused on personal history and identity throughout Southern California. Raquelle has been published in *BLACK-BERRY: A Magazine* (2012) and the Digging Deep, Facing Self anthology *Let the Head Remain* (2014), curated by Caits Meissner. They have been a participant in the Hurston/Wright Foundation Writers Weekend with Danez Smith and NYWC's Black Writers Program with Naomi Extra.

Ivanova Veras de Jesús (b. 1997, Dominican Republic) (*elle*/they) is a Black queer artist, activist, and researcher from the Dominican Republic. Art has been part of their life for as long as they can remember. Writing and theater have saved them and given them a home countless times. Ivanova is co-creator and co-host of a social justice and mental health podcast called "Hablamo' el Marte' RD." Additionally, they are a co-facilitator for QTPOC+ Family Circle, a Houston-based, welcoming, whole-identity-affirming space for Queer Trans People of Color and their families. Their research focuses on the neurocognitive and psychophysiological effects of stress, discrimination, and trauma within historically marginalized communities: specifically, on the ways these experiences impact mental and physical health as well as possible actions that can be taken to prevent and mitigate these effects. Ivanova deeply believes in the transformative power of love, art, accountability, and community.

Franchesca Araújo (b. 1998, United States) is an anticolonial writer centering oral histories, memories, and subjectivities outside of the documentation regime, and reading the world through the locus of the Caribbean. She's especially committed to the DR and Haiti as an insurgent island unit and to Black Dominican histories against dominant U.S. and hegemonic state elite narratives, based on valorization of Black aesthetics over materiality, collective relationships to bodies of water, and the Caribbean and Brazil in relation through amefricanidade.

Phoenix Rízing (b. 1995, United States) is an entrepreneur, writer, spoken-word poet, and motivational speaker from the South Bronx. She graduated from Marist College with a bachelor's in English writing. She is a U.S. Fulbright Alumna, Gates Millennium Scholar, John Lewis Fellowship Alumna, and NBCUniversal Page Program Alum. Phoenix Rízing's work can be found in the *Bronx Native Writer's Anthology*, *Into the Void*, *LUNA Magazine*, *We Are Antifa*, *Sad Girls Club Literary Blog*, the *Bronx Memoir Project Anthology Vol. 5*, and *Black Superwoman Chronicles.* In 2018, Darriel taught English in South Africa. In 2020, she was a Frost Place Conference on Poetry participant. As of 2021, she completed the Writers' Access Support Staff Training Program sponsored by the Writers Guild Foundation, as well as the DEAR Fellowship program for artists, and made it onto *Urban Arts Magazine*'s 2022 40 Under 40 in the Arts list. She is the author of the poetry book *The Ghetto Youth Handbook.*

Julia Feliz (b. 1982, Borikén / Puerto Rico) is a professional resource activist, content editor, writer, and illustrator with a background in science/research and over twenty-five years of experience (JuliaFeliz.com). Their authored work is taught in universities, cited by academics around the world, and, most importantly, read by all those working toward disrupting the settler system. Julia is also the founder of SanctuaryPublishers.com, a nontraditional book publisher focused on consistent anti-oppression, a

term they coined to help bridge social justice movements, and on raising voices. Among many other projects, they also founded the non-
profit NewPrideFlag.com as a call to center the most marginalized in the
2SLGBTQIA+ movement.

Jennifer Castillo (b. 1998, United States) is a literacy reading intervention-
ist in Denver, Colorado, and a first-generation college graduate in English
education from NYU Steinhardt's Teaching and Learning Department. Jennifer is an alum of the Youth Online Writer's Web. She is also a certified
English language arts and Spanish foreign-language teacher with the Colorado Board of Education. Jennifer is a first-generation American Bronxite
born in Washington Heights to a Dominican-Salvadoran family in New
York City. Jennifer has previously published collaboratively in May 2021 in
the *Journal of Language and Literacy Education* at the University of Geor-
gia, on role-playing games using social justice lenses in high-school English
classroom spaces. Jennifer's interests are in cultivating student agency and
interaction through reading and writing instruction, and exploring the
intersections of languages and multiple identities in learning spaces in her
writing and in new literacy studies.

Allison Whittenberg (b. 1976, United States) has a global perspective. If
she wasn't an author, she'd be a private detective or a jazz singer. Some of
her short stories are gathered in the collection *Carnival of Reality* (Appren-
tice, 2022). Whittenberg's novels are *Sweet Thang, Hollywood and Maine,
Life Is Fine,* and *Tutored* (Random House). Her upcoming collection of
poetry, *Driving with a Poetic License,* is out September 2024.

Irene Vázquez (b. 1998, United States) is a Black Mexican American poet,
journalist, and editor originally from Houston, Texas, the unceded territory
of the Karankawa and Ishak peoples. They write at the intersection of Black
cultural work, place-making, and the environment. Irene's debut chapbook,
Take Me to the Water, was released by Bloof Books in 2022. Irene is a Best
of the Net and Pushcart Prize nominated writer, whose work can be found
in *Muzzle,* the *Oxford American,* and the *Brooklyn Rail,* among others.
When not writing, Irene likes drinking coffee, watching the WNBA, and
reminding folks that the South has something to say.

Sasha Mahalia Hawkins (b. 1992, United States) (she/they) is a queer
multiethnic composer, sound designer, poet, and singer-songwriter. They

grew up in Europe and stateside through the U.S. military system, and their work is shaped by dissent and ideas of belonging and tenderness. Birth and postpartum studies, as well as their own spiritual journey, have highlighted the importance of dedicating their spiritual and artistic practices to nourishing the courage to heal what others in their line could not. They have released music as a solo artist and with their band Lady and the Lion, and are a proud founding board member of AlMonía Souls in Harmony, a queer community of spiritual creatives.

Edgie Amisial (b. 1998, United States) is a queer Haitian American writer and visual artist. She was born in Florida, United States, and raised in Port-au-Prince, Haiti. Growing up, storytelling helped her navigate her questions about her identity, her ancestry, and her world. She often wrote stories inspired by people she encountered in her daily life—people who she believed deserved to be remembered. After moving from Haiti to the United States at the age of eleven, she used painting and writing as tools to heal from intergenerational trauma, to release fears of not belonging, and to embrace her repressed sexuality. Since receiving a self-designed BA in arts and media activism from the New School, she has been using her creative practice to challenge systems of oppression, write stories that honor her memories of home, and highlight the trials and triumphs of existing as a queer Black woman.

Alejandro Heredia (b. 1994, Dominican Republic) is a queer Afro-Dominican writer and community organizer from the Bronx. He is a 2018 VONA/Voices Fellow and 2019 Dreamyard Rad(ical) Poetry Consortium Fellow. In 2019, he was selected by Myriam Gurba as the winner of the Gold Line Press Fiction Chapbook Contest. His book of short stories, *You're the Only Friend I Need* (2021), explores themes of queer transnationalism, friendship, and (un)belonging in the African diaspora. Alejandro's work has been featured in *Teen Vogue, Lambda Literary Review, Tasteful Rude Magazine*, and elsewhere.

Randy Markel James (b. 1984, United States) is an educator, editor, teacher, and performer from Los Angeles, California. James has studied writing at UCLA and USF (San Francisco). His work has been published in *Red Cedar Review, Palette, The Rumpus, Sepia Review*, and *Essential Truths: The Bay Area in Color*. James has performed in venues across Los Angeles and the San Francisco Bay Area. His chapbook, *Shifters*, is now available from Nomadic Press.

Charles Rice-González (b. 1964, Puerto Rico) is a writer, LGBTQ activist, co-founder of BAAD! The Bronx Academy of Arts and Dance, and an assistant professor at Hostos Community College. His novel, *Chulito*, received recognition from the American Library Association and the National Book Critics Circle, he co-edited *From Macho to Mariposa: New Gay Latino Fiction*, and his writing has been published in over a dozen anthologies. His play *I Just Love Andy Gibb* was published in *Blacktino Queer Performance: A Critical Anthology*. His honors include a MacDowell Fellowship, a Lannan Foundation Fellowship, a PEN America Writing as Activism Fellowship, awards from the NY City Council and *Gay City News* for his activism and contributions to advancing the lives of LGBTQ people, and a Lifetime Achievement Honor from the Bessies—NY Dance and Performance. He's the board chair for BCA and NALAC, and serves on the Macondo Writers Retreat advisory board.

des jackson (b. 2000, United States) is a Black Mexican American queer and current undergraduate at UC Berkeley, studying comparative literature, education, and African American studies. They are invested in the possibilities writing offers for liberation and have written poetry and prose from a very young age.

Josslyn Glenn (b. United States) (she/*ella*) is a Southern California–born Black Caribbean and Latina transgender producer, writer, spokesperson, and film festival programmer dedicated to promoting nuanced representations of queer and trans people of color, who have historically been under- and misrepresented in media. She is also the author of *She Rotates with Pluto: A Collection of Short Stories and Poems*. She has produced award-winning branded, editorial, scripted, and unscripted projects screening internationally, such as PeroLike's "Being Queer in the Trans Community," ABC's *Soul of a Nation Presents "Pride: To Be Seen"* and *Soul of a Nation Presents "The Freedom to Exist."* She has worked on the likes of Netflix's *Disclosure* and Con Todo's *Visions of Us*. When she is not craving nachos, she is writing her second book, *Tranny Pants*, a collection of diary entries, essays, interviews, poems, and short stories detailing the familial and romantic lives of trans people she has come across.

JR Mahung (b. 1992, United States) is a Garifuna poet from the South Side of Chicago. She now lives in Boston, Massachusetts, where she writes, meal preps, and works as an educator. JR's second collection of poems, *Since When He Have Wings*, is available through Pizza Pi Press.

Sr. Álida (b. 1988, Dominican Republic) is a queer Black writer and educator. Her work dissects ideas of identity—Blackness, queerness, womanhood, Dominicanidad, and language. A lover of Black people and malecón sunsets, when she's not teaching, she's most commonly found daydreaming about Caribbean Sundays. You can find her most recent publication in the 2021 summer issue of the *Southern Humanities Review* (vol. 54, no. 2). She is a 2021–2024 MFA candidate in fiction at the University of Mississippi.

SA Smythe (Jamaica / Costa Rica) is a poet, transdisciplinary artist, translator, and critical theorist committed to Black belonging beyond all borders and how archives of otherwise possibility come to be narrated and remembered. Smythe has written a collection of poetry, titled *proclivity*, about Black trans embodiment and a familial history of Black migration (between Jamaica, Britain, Costa Rica, and Italy). Their writing is featured in *The Feminist Wire, okayafrica, contemp(t)orary, Johannesburg Salon, Critical Contemporary Journal*, and several anthologies and edited volumes. Smythe has performed or exhibited performance and sound art at Kampnagel, Scuderie del Quirinale, the Museum of the African Diaspora, Centro nazionale di produzione Virgilio Sieni, GXRLSCHOOL, Polo del '900, and Mattatoio Museum, as a headliner for the Africa Writes Literary Festival in London, and elsewhere in collaborative and solo projects, installations, and festivals. They currently work as assistant professor of Black studies and the archive at the University of Toronto.

Breena Nuñez (b. 1989, United States) is a cartoonist and professor from the San Francisco Bay Area. She creates comics that center on the nuances of existing as an AfroCentral American person from the United States and articulate what queerness means to her as well. You can find some of Breena's journalism and memoir comics on *The Nib* and *The New Yorker: Daily Shouts*, and in anthologies like *Drawing Power: Women's Stories of Sexual Violence, Harassment, and Survival* and *Be Gay, Do Comics!*

Louie Ortiz-Fonseca (b. United States) (they/them) is an Afro–Puerto Rican queer storyteller living with HIV and the creator of Gran Varones (https://granvarones.com/).

Lorraine Avila (b. United States) (she/they) is a Bronxite with Caribbean roots in the Dominican Republic. Her mission is to break free from generational trauma by continuing to rupture traditions of silence. Avila is the author of *Malcriada and Other Stories* (DWA, 2019), *Celestial Summer* (2022), and *The Making of Yolanda La Bruja* (Levine Querido, 2023). Avila's writing has been published in *Refinery29, Teen Vogue, Bitch Media, Tasteful Rude, Our House LA, Latino USA, Catapult Magazine, Asteri(x) Journal, Hippocampus Magazine, Moko Magazine, The GirlMob, Acentos Review, La Galeria Magazine,* and *Blavity.*

Darrel Alejandro Holnes is an Afro-Panamanian American performer and writer and the author of *Stepmotherland* (Notre Dame Press, 2022) and *Migrant Psalms* (Northwestern Press, 2021). He is the recipient of the Andres Montoya Poetry Prize from Letras Latinas, the Drinking Gourd Poetry Prize, and a National Endowment for the Arts Literature Fellowship in Creative Writing (Poetry). His poem "Praise Song for My Mutilated World" won the C. P. Cavafy Poetry Prize from Poetry International. His writing has been published in English, Spanish, and French in literary journals, anthologies, and other books worldwide and online. He also writes for the stage and screen. Most of his writing centers on love, family, race, immigration, and joy. He works as a college professor in New York City. For more information, visit www.darrelholnes.com.

Yamilette Vizcaíno Rivera is a Dominican American writer and educator based in Brooklyn. She has received fellowships from the HUES Foundation and Sundress Academy for the Arts, and was the inaugural writer in residence at Velvet Park Media. A Tin House and VONA alum, her words can be found online at *Barrelhouse, Cosmonauts Avenue,* and *Liminal Transit Review.* Her chapbook "Little, Little, Little, Big, Big, Big" is available from the Hellebore Press, and she is hard at work on her novel.

Andrea Alejandro Freire F. // Drejanx (b. 1989, Ecuador) is a performer, butohka, cultural manager, and writer based in Guayaquil, an Ecuadorian port city. They are an HIV-positive queer activist and a member of the Furia collective, a platform for the dissemination of printed art and independent publishers through the international festival Furia Fanzine Fest. Andrea Alejandro serves as editor of Máquina Púrpura Ediciones, an independent publishing house that deals with crookedness, abject aesthetics, transfeminist thought, and gender-sex dissidence. They are also the coordinator at TrueQué Artistic Residency and the director of "Las Maricas no olvidamos," a space that works on the systematization, restoration, protection, editing, production, dissemination, and vindication of the sex-dissident archives in Ecuador. Andrea Alejandro is scriptwriter and host of La imagen parlante, a podcast about animated cinema produced by Radio UArtes.

Lawrence Schimel (b. 1971, United States) is a bilingual (Spanish/English) writer who has published over 120 books as author or anthologist, which have won him the Lambda Literary Award (twice), among many other honors. He is also a literary translator. Recent translations into English include *La Bastarda* by Trifonia Melibea Obono (US: Feminist Press; South Africa: Modjaji Books), the first novel by a woman writer from Equatorial Guinea to be published in English, and the poetry collection *Voice of the Two Shores* by Agnès Agboton (UK: flipped eye); into Spanish, South African poet Koleka Putuma's *Amnesia colectiva* (co-translated with Arrate Hidalgo; Spain: Flores Raras), George Takei's graphic novel memoir *Nos llamaron Enemigo* (US: Top Shelf), and Maggie Nelson's lyric essay *Bluets* (Spain: Tres Puntos).

Library of Congress Cataloging-in-Publication Data

Names: Pelaez Lopez, Alan, 1993– editor.

Title: When language broke open : an anthology of queer and trans Black writers of Latin American
descent / edited by Alan Pelaez Lopez.

Other titles: Camino del sol.

Description: Tucson : University of Arizona Press, 2023. | Series: Camino del sol: a Latinx literary
series

Identifiers: LCCN 2022058187 (print) | LCCN 2022058188 (ebook) | ISBN 9780816549962 (paperback) |
ISBN 9780816549979 (ebook)

Subjects: LCSH: Literature—Black authors—Literary collections. | Gender-nonconforming people's
writings. | Literature, Modern—21st century.

Classification: LCC PN6068 .W44 2023 (print) | LCC PN6068 (ebook) | DDC 808.8/992066—dc23/
eng/20230607

LC record available at https://lccn.loc.gov/2022058187

LC ebook record available at https://lccn.loc.gov/2022058188